Improving Learning Cultures in Further Education

Every year more than 3 million students are enrolled for full-time or part-time study at colleges of Further Education, and more than half of them are adults. Despite the sheer size of this sector, it has not been the object of much systematic, independent research. *Improving Learning Cultures in Further Education* presents the findings from a large-scale longitudinal research project into the practices of teaching and learning in Further Education (FE) and argues that there is much scope for improvement.

With a unique theoretical framework based on a cultural understanding of teaching and learning and focused on the formation and transformation of learning cultures, this book develops a new way of understanding educational improvement. The book is structured around three key questions:

- What do learning cultures in FE look like and how do they transform over time?
- How do learning cultures transform people?
- How can people (tutors, managers, policy-makers, but also students) transform learning cultures for the better?

Through a combination of theory, analysis and case studies, *Improving Learning Cultures in Further Education* makes a strong case for the importance of a cultural approach to the improvement of teaching and learning in Further Education and provides practical guidance for researchers, policy-makers and practitioners for implementing change for the better.

David James is Professor of Education at the University of the West of England, Bristol, and Visiting Professor at the Faculty of Education and Psychology, University of Latvia. He is a former FE teacher.

Gert Biesta is Professor of Education at the Institute of Education, University of Stirling and Visiting Professor for Education and Democratic Citizenship at Örebro University and Mälardalen University, Swed?

Improving Learning TLRP

Series Editor: Andrew Pollard, Director of the ESRC Teaching and Learning Research Programme

Improving Learning Cultures in Further Education

David James and Gert Biesta
with Helen Colley, Jennie Davies, Denis
Gleeson, Phil Hodkinson, Wendy Maull,
Keith Postlethwaite and Madeleine Wahlberg

Routledge
Taylor & Francis Group
New York   London

First published 2007
by Routledge
2 Park Square, Milton Park, Abingdon, Oxon OX14 4RN

Simultaneously published in the USA and Canada
by Routledge
270 Madison Avenue, New York, NY 10016

Routledge is an imprint of the Taylor & Francis Group, an informa business

British Library Cataloguing in Publication Data
A catalogue record for this book is available from the British Library

Library of Congress Cataloging in Publication Data
Improving learning cultures in further education /
edited by David James and Gert Biesta.
p. cm. – (Improving learning)
Includes bibliographical references and index.
ISBN 978-0-415-42735-7 – ISBN 978-0-415-42736-4 (pbk.)
1. Continuing education–Great Britain. 2. Adult education–Great Britain.
3. Adult learning–Great Britain. I. James, David, 1956– II. Biesta, Gert.
LC5256.G7147 2007
374.941–dc22
2007007586

ISBN13: 978-0-415-42736-4 (pbk)

For Martin Bloomer

Without his unselfish leadership, far-sighted intellectual vision and above all friendship, the research upon which this book is based would not have been carried out, and the book could not have been written.

Contents

List of project members

Graham Anderson was one of the Transforming Learning Cultures (TLC) project's four FE-based research fellows. He spent twenty-nine years teaching a wide range of business and economics courses in FE and was an advanced practitioner in business studies in a large urban college. He has taught learners from level 1 through to graduates. He particularly valued the opportunity that the project gave him to develop a critical and questioning stance in relation to teaching and learning in FE, and feels that the experience made him a better teacher and manager. He is now the director of a Chinese company offering A levels in eight centres in China.

Gert Biesta joined the TLC project team as a director in 2003. He is Professor of Education at the Institute of Education of the University of Stirling, Scotland. Since 2001 he has been Visiting Professor for Education and Democratic Citizenship at Örebro University and Mälardalen University, Sweden. He taught physics to radiographers, was a teacher educator and taught philosophy of education at several Dutch universities. In 1999 he moved to England. He has published widely on the relationships between education and democracy, the role of communication in education, theories of learning and education, the history of educational thought, and the philosophy and methodology of educational research. His empirical research focuses on democratic learning of young people and adults, lifelong learning, and teachers' professional learning.

Helen Colley was one of the project's five university-based research fellows until she moved from Leeds University to Manchester Metropolitan University (MMU) in October 2004, though she continued to work with the TLC project and write up some of its findings.

She is a senior research fellow at MMU, where she also teaches on postgraduate courses in research methods and supervises doctoral students. Her professional background is in career advice and guidance, supporting young people in inner-city schools in their transitions to Further Education and training. Her other research projects have focused on mentoring for social inclusion, informality and formality in learning, postgraduate student careers, and assessment for basic skills.

Jennie Davies was one of the five university-based research fellows in the TLC project, based at the University of Exeter. She is currently the lead research fellow for the Nuffield Foundation project Improving Formative Assessment in Vocational Education and Adult Literacy, Language and Numeracy. Her research interests include the learning experiences and formation of vocational aspirations of young people in FE. Before joining the TLC project, her background was in teaching, with considerable experience in secondary, further and adult education.

Kim Diment was one of the five university-based research fellows in the TLC project, based at the University of the West of England, Bristol. Her research interests include the teaching of Shakespeare and the use of drama, especially the use of performance as a research tool in working with students with learning difficulties and disabilities. She is currently a research fellow at the University of Exeter, working on a project about young people's career trajectories.

Denis Gleeson was one of the directors of the TLC project, and one of its original designers. He is Professor of Education at the University of Warwick, and has researched and published widely on post-compulsory education, training policy, management and professionalism in learning and skills sector. Recent and current research focuses on academy schools, leadership in FE and centres of vocational excellence.

Phil Hodkinson was one of the directors of the TLC project and one of its original designers. He is Professor of Lifelong Learning at the University of Leeds. He has researched and published widely on vocational education and training, career development and progression, and on workplace learning. He led the Leeds team in their work on the project.

David James was one of the TLC project's directors, and one of its original designers. His background includes leaving a secure and well-paid job in his mid-twenties to become a mature student, and gaining a degree and a teaching qualification. This launched his Further Education teaching career, and he taught on psychology, sociology, communication studies and professional development courses in FE colleges before moving into Higher Education HE at the end of the 1980s. He is Professor of Education at the University of the West of England, Bristol, and has published widely on research methodology, Further Education and assessment.

Wendy Maull was one of the five university-based research fellows on the project, based at the University of Exeter. Her main focus was on the quantitative data and its analysis. She has a background in mathematics education and has worked as a research fellow at the universities of Plymouth and Exeter. Her research interests include conceptual understanding of mathematics and the use of statistics to find patterns in large data sets, and she is currently providing quantitative methods support to the University of Exeter's Department of Management.

Keith Postlethwaite was one of the project's directors, and one of its original designers. He took particular responsibility for the quantitative data and analysis in the project. He taught physics to secondary pupils of all abilities for nine years, and then worked at the universities of Oxford, Reading and the West of England, before moving to the University of Exeter in 1999. Research interests include professional learning, science education (especially in relation to differentiation and able pupils) and the relevance of cultural theories of learning to these fields. In pursuing these interests he uses action research, quantitative methods and mixed methodologies.

Tony Scaife was one of the four college-based research fellows in the project. He is currently is enjoying work as a training consultant and part-time tutor on the Professional Studies in Teaching and Learning Foundation Degree in the Lifelong Learning Centre at the University of Leeds. In over forty years in Further Education he had a variety of roles: part-time student, tutor-librarian, staff development tutor, course tutor and curriculum development manager. He describes as 'transforming' the experience of working within the TLC project. Shortly before it ended he parted from his final college more convinced than ever that FE is a service in great need of tender loving care.

Michael Tedder was one of the four college-based research fellows in the project. He worked in Further Education for nearly thirty years, starting as a Liberal Studies lecturer and finding his way eventually to teacher education for further and adult education teachers. Always an advocate of the idea of teachers-as-researchers, he jumped at the chance to become involved in the TLC project. He was made redundant from his FE teaching post in the second year of the project. Since June 2004 he has been research fellow at Exeter University in another research project entitled Learning Lives: Learning, Identity and Agency in the Lifecourse. He completed his PhD in 2006.

Madeleine Wahlberg was one of the five university-based research fellows, based at the University of Warwick, where she continues to work in the Centre for Education and Industry. She is currently researching the Centres of Vocational Excellence programme in FE. Since 1992 she has been researching in many fields, mostly around different issues of public policy. Before that she spent seventeen years lecturing in the political economy of urbanism, and she was a practising town planner.

Eunice Wheeler was one of the four college-based research fellows. She is a teaching and learning development coordinator in an FE college and teaches on an in-service PGCE, Cert Ed (PCET) and BA Ed. After training in art and design she started working in FE, mainly in vocational and work-based training before moving into teacher training. Recent research has focused on workplace observation and she continues to support practitioner-based research through teacher training and the college's own Research Group.

Foreword

By Frank Coffield

This book is the fruit of the biggest research project ever carried out in the United Kingdom into Further Education (FE), a notoriously under-researched area. It is based on a case study approach of nineteen learning sites in four FE colleges, with the intensive participation of many FE teachers. It arrives at an opportune moment when the government and its principal agents (the Learning and Skills Council and the Quality Improvement Agency) are setting off in pursuit of excellence in the sector. But how is that to be achieved?

To understand the response of the researchers we need first to appreciate two of the key terms which hold this book and their project together: a cultural theory of learning and the notion of learning cultures. The former term conceives of learning, not as something that happens in the heads of students (or tutors), but as something that happens in and through social practices. The latter term, 'learning cultures', stands for the social practices through which people learn.

The importance of their approach lies in the challenge it offers many officially accepted assumptions about what constitutes good teaching and learning. Let me mention three examples. First, the assumption that learning is mainly an individual, cognitive process. Second, that 'good practice' is easily transferable to all sorts of different contexts. Third, that tutors are the only determinants of good teaching that matter. These three mistaken assumptions are, however, the basis of the government's model of reform.

If this book were to have just one major impact, I would want it to dispel forever the simple belief among politicians and policy-makers that the processes of teaching and learning and attempts to improve learning are merely technical matters. As the authors rightly argue there are no 'simple rules for action or recipes for effective teaching' (p. 20).

Let me briefly demonstrate the richness of their approach by contrasting their ideas for improvement with those offered by the final report of the Leitch (2006) review of skills in the United Kingdom. The researchers provide a sophisticated and detailed account of the characteristics of learning cultures and of six broad principles for improving learning. I have space here to mention only their four 'drivers for improvement'. First, they point to the need to engage the interests of students, which often go way beyond passing exams and getting jobs. Second, we should tap into the 'reservoir of tutor experience, altruism and professionalism' (p. 148). Third, 'a greater understanding of and support for excellent pedagogy . . . that is sensitive to the nature of the particular learning culture' (p. 149). Finally, we should take a cultural view of learning which would enhance the synergies between all positive aspects within an FE college.

What does Leitch offer in contrast? The review of skills 'identified five key factors that underpin a culture of learning' (Leitch 2006: 105), but then listed only four, which suggests that the national deficit in numeracy skills is more pervasive than was thought. The four factors identified are: raising the aspiration and motivation of individuals; keeping individuals fully informed; providing learners with choice; and offering financial support to those who need it. These suggestions are worthy, if rather predictable, but they also contain one fatal flaw: how is it possible to create 'a culture of learning' without an explicit and sophisticated notion of both 'learning' and of 'culture'? *Improving Learning Cultures in Further Education* contains both, as well as a convincing account of how they can be brought together in the interests of making students, tutors and institutions better at learning.

Frank Coffield
Institute of Education, University of London

Series editor's preface

The Improving Learning series showcases findings from projects within ESRC's Teaching and Learning Research Programme (TLRP) – the UK's largest ever coordinated educational research initiative.

Books in the Improving Learning series are explicitly designed to support 'evidence-informed' decisions in educational practice and policy-making. In particular, they combine rigorous social and educational science with high awareness of the significance of the issue being researched.

Working closely with practitioners, organisations and agencies covering all educational sectors, the Programme has supported many of the UK's best researchers to work on the direct improvement of policy and practice to support learning. Over sixty projects have been supported, covering many issues across the lifecourse. We are proud to present the results of this work through books in the Improving Learning series.

Each book provides a concise, accessible and definitive overview of innovative findings from a TLRP investment. If more advanced information is required, the books may be used as a gateway to academic journals, monographs, websites, etc. On the other hand, shorter summaries and research briefings on key findings are also available via the Programme's website at www.tlrp.org.

We hope that you will find the analysis and findings presented in this book are helpful to you in your work on improving outcomes for learners.

Andrew Pollard
Director, Teaching and Learning Research Programme
Institute of Education, University of London

Preface

This book is based on the Transforming Learning Cultures in Further Education project, which ran from 2001 to 2005 and was part of the Teaching and Learning Research Programme overseen by the Economic and Social Research Council (ESRC: Reference L139251025). The project brought together a number of distinctive ideas, perspectives and people. More than any other factor, Martin Bloomer's leadership created the right environment to bring out the complementarity of these contributions and it set the tone for a collective endeavour that was highly productive. Martin continues to be sorely missed following his untimely death in 2002.

The project represented the first ever large-scale, independent study of teaching and learning in Further Education in England. From conception through to completion it included a serious effort to build partnerships between researchers and practitioners. It was underpinned by a wish to research *with* rather than *on* FE and a conviction that the authentic study of learning and teaching – rather than their reduction to predetermined variables – would be the most likely route to useful knowledge.

The book has two lead authors and its chapters have a total of nine authors, but at the same time it represents the culmination of a broader and sustained team effort. By way of example, the analysis of interventions discussed in Chapter 6 draws upon materials and extended discussions to which all members of the team made extensive contributions. The team members are listed, with brief biographical details, at the start of this book.

Improving Learning Cultures in Further Education is intended to provide a gateway to the project rather than a fully comprehensive account of it. This has given us some difficult decisions about what data and analysis to leave out. One immediately apparent effect is that some of the nineteen 'learning sites' are more visible than others. However, we resisted the temptation to engineer a common density of coverage because we felt that this would obscure some of the most important arguments in the book while offering only a spurious completeness of coverage. We hope that the result, in which readers will meet some of the learning sites several times but in different ways, assists rather than hinders understanding.

David James and Gert Biesta

Acknowledgements

We would like to thank all members of the TLC project team for their help in bringing this book to fruition. We are also immensely grateful to the wider team involved – to the college-based participating tutors who we cannot name directly but who often appear in the text via their pseudonyms, and their students, who gave so generously of their time to participate in the research. Hilary Olek, the project administrator, deserves particular praise for her organisational contribution to the project. The Teaching and Learning Research Programme provided a series of challenges, opportunities and encouragements, and we would particularly like to thank Andrew Pollard, Kathryn Ecclestone, Stephen Baron, Jenny Shackleton and David Raffe for their part in these.

Part I

What are the issues?

Chapter 1

Improving learning cultures in Further Education?

Introduction

Is there scope for improvement in Further Education? Many people, from politicians and policy-makers to college managers and FE tutors, believe there is. As a matter of fact the pursuit of improvement is one of the few constant factors in the history of the sector. It is, of course, not only students who 'can do better' – the question of improvement is relevant for all who are involved in the creation of opportunities for learning, either directly or indirectly. But improvement is a difficult concept. What does it mean to improve? And how can it actually be done? This is partly a normative question, since any discussion about improvement requires value judgements about what counts as improvement. Is it improvement when more students get a qualification? Is it improvement when more students are happy? Is it improvement when a course becomes more selective? Is it improvement when tutors replace teaching with assessment? The question of improvement also has a political dimension which has to do with who is allowed to participate in making such value judgements. Should this be the prerogative of tutors? College management? Funding bodies? Inspectors? The government? Students?

There are also many practical questions around improvement. After all, even if there is agreement about what *should* happen, there are still different ways in which this might be achieved and different places to start from. Traditionally there has been a strong emphasis on teaching as the main driver of learning and the main motor of improvement. But although teaching is important, there are many other factors that impact

Authored by David James, Gert Biesta, Phil Hodkinson, Keith Postlethwaite and Denis Gleeson

upon the learning opportunities and the actual learning of students. Good teaching does influence learning, but it does not determine it. In this book we therefore advance a different approach to the question of improvement, one which aims to capture the complex interaction between the many factors, dimensions and influences that shape the learning opportunities for students. Our approach is informed by a *cultural understanding of learning*, and the key notion in this approach is the idea of a *learning culture*. Learning cultures are the social practices through which people learn.

Our answer to the question of improvement is in a sense very simple: *Change the culture!* But this is more easily said than done. This is first of all because learning cultures are complex and multifaceted entities. One might be able to influence some of the factors that shape a particular learning culture, but many factors are beyond the control of those directly involved, either because they are under the control of others (the funding of Further Education is, for example, beyond the control of tutors) or because they are difficult to control anyway (think, for example, of the influence of social class and gender). Changing the culture is also difficult because it is people who make cultures. Even under virtually identical circumstances – for example students who take the same course, read the same books, get the same teaching and do the same assignments – students will have different experiences and will learn different things, partly because they are positioned differently within the learning culture, and partly because they come from different backgrounds, have different prior experiences and different access to resources. Thus learning cultures exist through the actions, dispositions and interpretations of the participants. They exist through interaction and communication and are (re)produced by individuals just as much as individuals are (re)produced by learning cultures. Individuals' actions are therefore neither totally determined by learning cultures nor totally free. This implies that we should not try to replace the question how teaching determines learning with the question how learning cultures determine learning. Our focus rather is on *learning opportunities*. The cultural approach to learning aims to understand the kinds of learning that are made possible as a result of the configuration of a particular learning culture, and the kinds of learning that become difficult or even impossible as a result of the way in which a particular learning culture operates. What we also should not forget in our attempts to change learning cultures, is that learning cultures are not static. They are social practices that depend on what people do and are therefore subject to continuous change (which explains why it often requires quite a lot of effort to keep learning cultures relatively stable over time), although the learning cultures of specific sites may differ in the extent of their openness to modification.

These considerations are captured in the title of the research project on which this book is based: Transforming Learning Cultures in Further Education (the TLC project). In one respect this title expresses the ambition of the TLC project to contribute to the improvement of learning in Further Education by focusing on the ways in which learning cultures can be transformed for the better. In another respect it acknowledges the ways in which learning cultures can be transforming for the teachers and students who participate in and contribute to them. The title also reveals our awareness that learning cultures in FE are themselves always 'in transformation' – and if there is one thing that our research has made visible, it is the extraordinary high pace of change in the Further Education sector.

To adopt a cultural approach to the improvement of learning in Further Education requires three things. First, it requires an understanding of the characteristics and dynamics of learning cultures in Further Education and of the wider contextual issues and developments in the sector, including an understanding of its history. It is, after all, only after we know what it is that we might want to transform that we can begin to think about transformation for improvement. Second, it requires an understanding of the dynamics of particular learning cultures and, more specifically, the relationships between learning cultures, learning opportunities, learning practices and learning 'outcomes'. We need, in other words, an understanding of the kinds of learning that are made possible as a result of the particular configuration of a learning culture and the kinds of learning that are made difficult or even impossible as a result of the way in which a particular learning culture operates. Third, we need to understand the ways in which learning cultures can be transformed and particularly the opportunities that the different actors in Further Education – from policy-makers and college management to tutors and students – have to influence, change and transform learning cultures. The chapters in this book are precisely organised along these lines.

First, we provide an overview of the theory of learning and the theory of learning cultures which have informed our research (Chapter 2). After this we sketch a brief history of improvement in the Further Education sector (Chapter 3) and provide an analysis of key characteristics of the learning cultures that we examined in our project (Chapter 4). We then address the question of how learning cultures transform people. We look at the practices of learning that result from deliberate attempts to organise learning cultures in a particular way ('the learning of practices'), and pay attention to how learning cultures shape people's thinking and doing in ways that are often less visible and sometimes even invisible from the perspective of the official curriculum ('the practices of learning') (Chapter 5). Next we focus on the question of how – and to what extent – learning cultures can deliberately be managed and transformed (Chapter 6) and we look at the wider (policy) context for professional action in Further Education (Chapter 7). Finally in Chapter 8 we discuss the practical implications of our research which we have summarised in a set of 'principles of procedure' which identify what policy-makers, college managers, tutors and students might do to transform learning cultures in Further Education for the better. In the remainder of this chapter we introduce the TLC project itself.

A quick reading guide

- If you read this book *from cover to cover* you will get a *detailed account of the Transforming Learning Cultures in Further Education project*, its theoretical framework, the main findings and conclusions and practical implications.
- If you are interested in the *practical implications* you can go to *Chapter 8* and have a look at the *Principles of Procedure* for improving learning and teaching in Further Education.
- If you want to read about the *theoretical framework* which underlies our work, you need to read *Chapter 2*.
- *Chapters 4, 5 and 6* give an *overview of our findings* and focus on the relationships between learning cultures, learning opportunities, learning practices and learning outcomes and show you how learning cultures might be transformed.
- *Chapters 3, 5 and 7 discuss underlying issues* that have to do with the ways in which learning cultures in FE can be transformed.
- The *Methodological Appendix* provides detailed information about how the project was designed and conducted and how we reached our conclusions.

The 'Transforming Learning Cultures In Further Education' project

The TLC project was announced in September 2000 as part of the second phase of the Teaching and Learning Research Programme, a large programme of research managed by the Economic and Social Research Council. The project started in 2001 and finished in 2005. To date it has been the biggest project ever targeted at English Further Education, a significantly under-researched sector. The project had three overarching aims:

- to deepen understanding of the complexities of learning in FE
- to identify, implement and evaluate strategies for the improvement of learning opportunities in FE
- to set in place an enhanced and lasting capacity among FE practitioners for inquiry into FE practice.

These challenging aims led us to adopt a relatively complex, large-scale research design which combined work on detailed case studies with extensive questionnaire surveys over a three-year data collection period. The project was conducted in a unique partnership between Higher Education academics and researchers from four universities and FE practitioners and researchers from four FE colleges – a decision motivated by the desire to conduct research *in* and *with* rather than *on* Further Education (see Bloomer and James 2003).

The context of the research

From its conception, the project recognised that English FE was chronically under-researched (Elliott 1996b; Hughes et al. 1996), especially when compared to other sectors. Most existing research focused on management and professional identity, rather than on learning (Elliott 1996a; Ainley and Bailey 1997; Gleeson and Shain 1999; Shain and Gleeson 1999). Some partial exceptions to this appeared in the public domain soon after the start of the project, including Ecclestone's work on particular forms of assessment (for example, Ecclestone 2002) and the work of Bathmaker and her colleagues on trainee FE teachers (for example, Bathmaker et al. 2002). Yet, despite this overall paucity of research, FE was nevertheless in a process of becoming more visible and significant in relation to government policy on lifelong learning, social inclusion and economic regeneration (Department for Education and Employment (DfEE) 1998, 1999; Department for Education and

Skills (DfES) 2003a, 2003b), and in the lives of vast numbers of young people and adults (Gleeson 1999).

This elevation of the profile of FE was accompanied by the creation of new structures and a redefined sector. Following the Learning and Skills Act 2000, the Further Education Funding Council was replaced in April 2001 by the Learning and Skills Council, with a much broader remit (essentially, post-16 learning of all kinds except Higher Education) and a national and regional structure: the new Learning and Skills Sector included work-based and adult and community providers in addition to colleges. The Further Education Development Agency (FEDA), with whom the TLC project had formed a partnership, itself dated from a merger in 1995 of the Further Education Unit and the national FE Staff College. It grew and changed a number of times internally and then in November 2000 became the Learning and Skills Development Agency (LSDA), a body which itself commissioned some new research with a bearing on learning in FE colleges (see, for example, LSDA 2003; Torrance et al. 2005), but compared to primary, secondary and higher education, the sector was and continues to be under-researched. It remains to be seen whether this situation changes under the most recent wave of reorganised structures. From April 2006 the Learning and Skills Development Agency divided into two new bodies: the Learning and Skills Network (LSN), responsible for research, training and consultancy, and the Quality Improvement Agency for Lifelong Learning (QIA), 'set up to spark fresh enthusiasm for innovation and excellence in the learning and skills sector' and to promote improvement through self-evaluation (QIA 2006). The LSDA also sponsored a regional network of researchers and practitioners – the Learning and Skills Research Network – which has continued to promote research activity in post-compulsory education despite the end of the LSDA. In addition, two other bodies now have a significant presence, in the form of Lifelong Learning UK (LLUK) and the Institute for Learning (IfL). The former body oversees the professional development of all those working in libraries, archives and information services, work-based learning, HE, FE and community learning and development; the latter one is, at the time of writing, working to establish itself as a membership-driven professional body for teachers and trainers and student teachers in the learning and skills sector. A further significant development is the move to 'demand-led' training where this means employer, not student, demand. This is being overseen by the Sector Skills Councils and includes a new engagement with both the structure and curricular content of all vocational training.

Because of its historical Cinderella-like image, the sheer scale of FE can be easily overlooked. At the time of our initial fieldwork, there were 2.35 million students enrolled at colleges in the FE sector in England, 1.97 million of whom were within Further Education Funding Council (FEFC) funded provision. Of these, 27.2 per cent of students were aged under 19; on average each of these students was studying for 3.49 qualifications, and 78.5 per cent of these were enrolled on full-time, full-year programmes. The qualifications for which they were studying were mainly vocational (the General National Vocational Qualification: GNVQ), as well as many qualifications focused on specific vocational areas. However, a significant number of full-time students were studying for academic qualifications at two levels: the General Certificate of Secondary Education (GCSE), normally intended for 16-year-old school leavers, and the more advanced General Certificate of Education (GCE) Advanced (A levels) and recently introduced half-A levels (AS). A total of 72.8 per cent of students on state-funded provision, then organised through the FEFC, were adults studying, on average, 1.32 qualifications each. Only 9.4 per cent of these adults were enrolled on a full-time, full-year programme. The qualifications for which they were working were very varied, with no one qualification standing out as by far the largest category (Learning and Skills Council (LSC) 2002).

This diversity of provision is visible in college-to-college variation and also across the range of activity within individual colleges. While this presented the project with a difficult set of decisions in terms of what to study, it also presented an opportunity, because we felt that if our cross-section of cases could reflect the diversity itself, this was likely to add to empirical and theoretical understanding of learning more generally. As is explained more fully in the chapters that follow, throughout the time of our research, the FE sector was (and arguably, still is) characterised and perhaps dominated by what has been termed the 'new managerialism' (Avis et al. 1996) or the audit culture (Power 1997). Following the Further and Higher Education Act 1992, colleges of Further Education moved out of the control of the local democratic structures and became free-standing in relation to a central government funding mechanism. This was called 'Incorporation'. The government subsequently established the FEFC together with a performance-related funding mechanism (Ainley and Bailey 1997). In essence, all state FE funding depended upon the recruitment, retention and achievement of individual students. A key focus of the new mechanism, especially in the early days, was to even out funding across all colleges, primarily by driving funding levels down, in a search for greater efficiency and 'value for money'. This was further supported, soon after, by the imposition of a national inspection service, which laid down detailed criteria against which FE provision was to be judged. Once the Labour government came to power in 1997, this audit trend continued, but with the added imperative to meet every student's personal learning needs and to increase social inclusion through widening participation.

As well as forming part of the context for the study, these factors have also impinged in a more intimate sense on the operation of the TLC, as will be briefly described later. They certainly provided a further justification for the research. There was a need to know how these processes, ostensibly aimed at improving learning, actually impacted upon learning and teaching on the ground. Furthermore, lying behind both the funding and inspection frameworks lurks a set of strong if implicit assumptions – that good teachers and teaching are always the prime determinants of effective learning, and that there are universally applicable standards of good teaching that can be applied in any situation. These assumptions are well worth testing out and the TLC research has provided the opportunity to do that.

The research context for the project was also significant. In the late 1990s, there was what appeared to be a concerted attack on educational research quality in the United Kingdom. This came from both inside the educational academic community (Hargreaves 1996, 1997; Reynolds 1998; Tooley and Darby 1998) and from outside (Hillage et al. 1998; Blunkett 2000; Oakley 2000). The main thrust of this attack was that too much educational research was of low quality, projects were too small and too diverse, there was little evidence of cumulative findings, and what there was lacked relevance to practice. In addition, it was argued that there was not enough quantitative research, and too much qualitative research lacked methodological rigour and transparency. Although most of the research being criticised related to school-based education, the cumulative impact of these challenges resulted in a significant shift in the climate for all educational research – towards a search for decontextualised scientific truths, telling government and practitioners 'what works' (see Hammersley 1997, 2002; Simons et al. 2003; Hodkinson 2004; Hodkinson and Smith 2004; Biesta 2007; for critiques of this 'new orthodoxy'). The Teaching and Learning Research Programme was at the vanguard of this new climate. At least in the early days, programme events celebrated research that might underpin the 'evidence-based practice' similar to that of the medical world and encouraged a perception that projects had to combine the scientific robustness of positivism, with the engagement of action research, all on a very large scale. Because of its scale and political significance, the TLRP and the projects within it had and continue to have a high profile.

The theoretical rationale for the project

One of the concerns of the TLRP was the need for the study of teaching and learning in 'authentic' ways. This idea resonated strongly with the collective view of the TLC team. We wished to study learning as it actually happened, and we were aware that this meant a departure from how learning was often defined, understood, measured and studied. But as our design-phase discussions with a range of FE practitioners continually underlined for us, 'authenticity' meant even more than this. An authentic study of learning must try to address the complexity of relationships between teachers, teaching, learners, learning, learning situations and the wider contexts of learning. Where educational research focuses on particular variables and, especially where these are narrowly defined, there is always a danger of decontextualising the object of study. Particular aspects are emphasised, often from within the concerns of one academic discipline, and other factors may come to be treated as background or even ignored. A well-known example would be the textbook presentation of classical and operant conditioning, offered to teachers and would-be teachers as a source of secure knowledge about the nature of learning. Our view is that teaching and learning cannot be decontextualised from broader social, economic and political forces, both current and historic, and that addressing this complexity directly is the most likely route to acquiring an understanding that will be useful to policy and practice.

In the TLC, we attached importance to the term 'culture' to indicate these complex relationships (see Chapter 2 for a more detailed explanation). The project aimed to examine, within a variety of settings, what a culture of learning is, based upon an acceptance that 'learning and thinking are always situated in a cultural setting, and always dependent upon the utilization of cultural resources' (Bruner 1996: 4). We conceptualised learning broadly within a situated learning frame, which sees learning as located in the interactions between context, concept and activity (Brown et al. 1989). Learning is an inseparable part of social practice (Lave and Wenger 1991), closely related to what might be termed the culture of the place of learning. Significant weight is given to informal as well as formal attributes of learning (Colley et al. 2003a).

One of the very few recent studies directly focused on learning in FE (Bloomer and Hodkinson 2000) found that students' dispositions

towards learning were intricately related to their wider social lives, both
inside and outside the college setting. In other words, there were strong,
even dominant cultural dimensions to those dispositions. These cultural
dimensions were partly related to the nature of the particular institution attended (Hodkinson and Bloomer 2000). Furthermore, for many
students, dispositions changed over a three-year period, centred around
their time in FE. However, this study did not investigate the links
between the dispositions of students and their learning, or examine
relationships between their changing dispositions and their learning
experiences and encounters in the FE colleges they attended. It also did
not take account of the dispositions and learning of teachers, implicitly
seeing colleges as sites where only students learned. This work led us
to recognise the need for a study directly focused on the nature of learning cultures that would identify aspects of those cultures amenable to
intervention at various levels. To help conceptualise this, we turned
to the work of Pierre Bourdieu (for example, Bourdieu 1977, 1989,
1998; Bourdieu and Wacquant 1992; Grenfell and James 1998). There
were five principal reasons for this orientation.

First, Bourdieu's theory-as-method offers researchers a relational
approach to social practices. Developing a distinction made by Ernst
Cassirer, Bourdieu contrasts relational with substantialist thinking: the
latter treats the preferences and activities of individuals or groups as
if they indicate an essence, while the former sees them as instances of
the intersection of relationships and positions in social space (see, for
example, Bourdieu 1998: 4). Earlier work within the team had shown
that this distinction had practical, as well as theoretical implications
(for example, James 1995).

Second, and closely related to this, the approach emphasises the
mutual interdependence of social constraint and individual volition,
or 'structure' and 'agency'. Social practices are understood as having
both an objective and a subjective reality at one and the same moment.
Complex human relations and activities can be understood via theoretical tools that enable the 'unpacking' of social practices in social spaces:
examples of these 'tools' include the notions of *habitus* (i.e. a collection
of durable, transposable dispositions) and *field* (a set of positions and
relationships defined by the possession and interaction of different
amounts of economic, social and cultural capital). Habitus and field are
mutually constituting, a point of significance for the way that the actions
of tutors, students and institutions are studied and understood. Put
more concretely, our assumption was that learning would depend upon
the complex interactions between the following factors, among others:

- students' positions, dispositions and actions, influenced by their previous life histories
- tutors' positions, dispositions and actions, influenced by their previous life histories
- the nature of the subject content, including broader issues of 'disciplinary identity' and status, as well as specifics such as syllabus, assessment requirements, links with external agencies or employers, etc.
- college management approaches and procedures, together with organisational structures, site location and resources
- national policies towards FE, including qualification, funding and inspection regimes
- wider social, economic and political contexts, which interpenetrate all of the other points.

Thinking relationally in the project meant seeing 'learning' in relation to people, organisations, times and places (for example, Who? When? Where?); in other words, the field site or context. Rather than taking the validity or utility of specific individual definitions of learning at face value, one might seek to understand them in terms of their location among a series of possible socially positioned definitions and in relation to other definitions in use.

Third, we had a wish to work across discipline boundaries. A Bourdieusian approach promotes a questioning stance in relation to the 'capture' of certain questions by particular academic disciplines, and as such has strong parallels in socio-cultural theory (for example, Wertsch 1998) and in cultural studies (for example, Smith 2000). A degree of interdisciplinarity would help the project to focus on its object of study (i.e. learning in a particular institutional context as a set of practices to be understood, explained or transformed). Given the dominance of some pre-existing models of learning, this was an important consideration.

Fourth, a Bourdieusian approach necessitates a robust form of reflexivity, which we felt was in keeping with the goals of the project, for example, keeping in view the relative social positionings of researchers and those they study, and the implications of this for knowledge generation. It also meant questioning the very research questions for the project and the wider programme that we were attempting to answer, in particular why, how, and in whose interests the need to improve teaching and learning in Further Education was being posed.

Finally, we were attracted by the possibility that Bourdieu's 'theory-as-method' and in particular the stance it promotes in relation to culture, could bring fresh insight to bear on the understanding of educational issues and settings (Grenfell and James 1998). However, having detailed these reasons for a particular theoretical orientation, it is important to note that theoretical work in the project does not limit itself to Bourdieusian tools. Our ideas about learning cultures and a cultural understanding of learning also draw, for example, on the work of John Dewey and Jean Lave and Etienne Wenger, as well as on critical feminist theory and thinkers such as Arlie Russell Hochschild, Beverley Skeggs and Inge Bates.

Project design and data-collection

In the TLC project we adopted a nested case-study approach to organise our data-collection. Four FE colleges were selected, and the design of the project negotiated with their principals and key staff. Each college was paired with one of the four host universities in the project. The colleges are of different types, serving different areas and communities, in different parts of England. At the second level, within each college, four specific sites of learning and teaching were identified, providing sixteen initial sites across the whole project. By 'site' we meant a location where tutor(s) and students worked together on learning. Site selection depended on negotiations between the research team and college management, and on the willingness of the tutor concerned to participate. Beyond that, we looked for variety of coverage, so that some sites resemble conventional classrooms, others workshops or workplaces, and others drop-in centres or distance learning. Sites also cover a range of different types of course provision, at different levels of qualification. As might be expected, there was some change to sites during the life of the project, which had the effect of increasing the overall number of cases within the project to a total of nineteen.

The nineteen learning sites of the TLC project (in alphabetical order)

- Access students individual tutoring (from September 2003 – replacing 'mature students support' – see below)

- Business Studies General National Vocational Qualification (GNVQ) intermediate level – one-year, level 2 course
- CACHE Diploma (Child Care and Education) – a two-year level 3 course, formerly known as 'nursery nursing'
- 'Connect 2', an entry level course for school leavers with moderate learning and behavioural difficulties
- Drama (Entry Level Drama) – a one- or two-year entry level course in drama production for students with learning difficulties, leading to an Award Scheme Development and Accreditation Network (ASDAN) Expressive Arts award
- Engineering in Electronics and Telecommunications (National Certificate, two years, day release)
- English for Speakers of Other Languages (ESOL) Learning Services (roll-on, roll-off)
- French Advanced Supplementary (AS) level (from September 2002)
- Health Studies Business and Technician Education Council (BTEC) National Diploma – a two-year course
- Information Technology (IT) skills by flexible learning (City and Guilds 7261) (2001–2002 only)
- Information Technology GNVQ (replacing the one above, from September 2002)
- Mature students support (up to September 2003) – one-to-one tutoring in a learning centre for students needing support in maths, English or study skills in relation to dyslexia
- Online basic IT skills
- Pathways for parents (re-engagement course for young parents)
- Photography (BTEC + City and Guilds; one and two years full or part time)
- Psychology AS level (2001–2002 only)
- Travel and Tourism Advanced Vocational Certificate of Education (AVCE) – a one- or two-year course
- Vocational course for Key Stage 4 (KS4) school students, replacing one of their GCSEs with a college course in Administration/ Information Technology
- Work-based NVQ Assessment in Administration, business and technology, NVQs, levels 2–3.

This selection is not representative of the whole of FE provision, though it is worth noting that its statistical profile is very close to the national (English) picture for FE as a whole, particularly in terms of gender, age and mode of study. More important, we were confident that it encompassed a good deal of the considerable diversity of the sector, and a wide enough range to allow for the identification of significant variations between sites or significant common issues across them. It is evident that HE provision is under-represented. Also, there is a slight preponderance of newer, almost experimental provision, because of the interest in examining this by some partner colleges. The main tutor in each site was funded for two hours a week, to participate in the research. These 'participating tutors' attended regular meetings and workshops with their host university/college research team, were encouraged to keep reflective log books or diaries, and to observe each other's sites. They were encouraged to innovate as the research progressed and, where new approaches were attempted, the research provided ongoing evidence of what happened. Engaging with them as partners, combined with legitimate college interests in not letting research near their poor provision, has no doubt given a slight 'positive bias' in the overall TLC sample. The tutors were mainly full-time, experienced and relatively enthusiastic, and overall teaching standards appeared to be high. As will become apparent in later chapters, it can be argued that this slight positive bias lends extra weight to the idea that the TLC findings have a wide applicability.

In addition to the participating tutors, each of the four local research teams had three core members:

- one of the project directors, nominally for one day per week
- a half-time academic researcher, employed by the university
- an FE practitioner/researcher, seconded for two days a week to work on the project.

The local research teams met approximately once per month. In addition to working with the participating tutors, the core researchers interviewed around six students per site twice a year, using semi-structured interviews, and observed the activity in each site on regular occasions. The observations in the project were quite different from those already common in the sector, which were designed to express judgements about teaching quality (potentially linked to pay and contracts) structured around a narrow set of criteria. Within the research, observation (sometimes termed 'shadowing') was based on a wide and fluid set of questions. It was concerned to find out what was going on, rather than to evaluate whether this met audit measures. Core researchers and visiting participating tutors recorded, in some detail, their impressions of the practices and settings in the sites. Participating tutors were also regularly interviewed, and gave periodic feedback about what the research showed about their particular site, and more general issues across the project as a whole. In addition to the qualitative case studies, the TLC also used regular questionnaire sweeps, to generate a broader picture of the sites. One director (nominally one day per week) and one half-time researcher worked exclusively on this part of the project. We aimed for as close to 100 per cent coverage of students in each site as we could get. Actual response rates varied from site to site, but the survey allowed us to contextualise the students who were intensively followed up by interview, and helped reveal patterns of similarity and difference between the sites. (For a more detailed account of data-collection and analysis see the Methodological Appendix at the end of this book.) We collected data over a period of three years. This allowed us to follow up to three cohorts in some sites. Some of the courses we studied ran for two years, whereas others ran for only one year or less.

How representative was our sample of students?

From the quantitative data collected through our survey sweeps we established two important points about the sites that formed part of the project. First, our data helped us to see how the characteristics of students in our sites related to those of students in FE generally, as mapped by national statistics. Broadly, our sample contained rather more full-time students than is the case nationally, and rather more students in the 14–19 age group: it contained fewer than expected older, part-time students. In terms of gender there was quite a close match to national data. In terms of ethnicity, our sample was mainly White British, again matching national statistics. This broad match between our samples and the national picture may reassure readers who wish to apply our findings to their own context. Second, we could compare our interviewees with the other students in their learning sites. This revealed that the interviewees were not distinctly different from the rest of the students in terms of these

continued

basic demographics. This may reassure readers that our qualitative insights were derived from students who (at least in these terms) were fairly typical of their site. More information can be found in the Methodological Appendix at the end of this book.

Data analysis

In approaching the analysis of data, we faced some difficult problems, each of which is also a source of strength. The data-collection generated a huge amount of data that enabled us to construct rich pictures of learning cultures in FE, but which also threatened to overwhelm us. By the conclusion of the project we had data from six questionnaire sweeps, about 600 student interviews, 100 tutor interviews, 16 log books, about 700 sets of observation notes, notes from local team meetings and discussions, interviews with a small number of college managers, and a large amount of documentary material. Initially, the quantitative and qualitative data were analysed separately. They were then integrated through an iterative process, between each major sweep of data collection. In analysing the quantitative data, we explored differences among sites, mapped changes in expectations over time, related expectations to perceived outcomes, and looked for relationships between sets of variables. For the qualitative data, we used each site as the main unit of analysis. After the first round of data collection, a detailed case study account was produced for each site. As the project progressed, case studies were updated progressively, focusing on deepening understanding, mapping change, and examining in depth the impact of various interventions into site culture – either initiated by the participating tutors or externally imposed.

As a first step in moving beyond individual case studies, the research teams responsible for each site produced short summaries of each case study to enable the whole team to share an understanding of all the sites without being swamped by detail. Through scrutiny of these summaries, and whole team discussion based on them, we addressed some broad themes drawing on data from the project as a whole. These themes reflected the issues which emerged as important in individual case studies yet also found resonance with data produced by other members of the team. In addition, we produced two analytical tools to enable us to address two key issues defined for the project as a whole:

the analysis of learning cultures and the analysis of interventions. In each case researchers responsible for each site were encouraged to search their data for insights into particular issues. The working papers produced by the teams were analysed and debated by the whole team at team meetings.

The integration of insights from the qualitative and quantitative strands of the project was achieved, at the simplest level, through regular comment from the researchers responsible for the quantitative work on drafts of all kinds of qualitative analysis. However, the quantitative work also explored groupings of sites, and the differences between these groupings. This formed the basis for an interrogation of the qualitative data for factors that might help to explain the position of a site in the overall analysis.

The participating tutors were all involved in the development of the case studies of their site. To enable understanding of the power relations in each site we decided from the outset, however, that participating tutors would not be involved in interviewing students and that we would not share with them the raw data from student interviews. Instead, we discussed sites informally with the participating tutors, and sometimes shared draft written accounts of the site with them. Participating tutors' comments on these drafts were treated as additional data through which the case study could be deepened. This approach recognised that participating tutors were both involved in the research and, at the same time, subjects of it. Despite the practical difficulties, there were also real strengths in this unusual relationship. We were able to collect data from students that might not have been made available to tutors as researchers. We also gained important insights from tutor diaries, meetings and discussions. The tutors, on the other hand, gained a greater understanding of FE and of teaching and learning, and some utilised the opportunity to rethink aspects of their practice, and to introduce changes, directly as a result of research involvement (see Anderson et al. 2003; see also James 2004). It also meant that tutors maintained control of their own teaching practices.

Conclusion: research in Further Education

One of the main ambitions of the TLRP programme is that research should directly improve teaching and learning or, to put it slightly more realistically, make a positive impact on teaching and learning practices. One way in which we have tried to contribute to this aim in the TLC project was through a deliberate effort not to conduct research *on* Further Education but to locate the research firmly *in* Further Education (for this distinction, see Bloomer and James 2003) and conduct it together *with* those working in the sector. This was the reason why the project had four participating tutors and a part-time college-based research fellow from each college as well as five university-based research fellows. Participation in the project definitely had an impact on the college-based team members– we have documented part of this learning process in a separate publication called *Research in Practice: Experiences, insights and interventions from the project Transforming Learning Cultures in Further Education* (James 2004). Having an impact on others in the participating colleges and beyond has been more of a challenge, though the project can point to some demonstrable 'impacts' at college and sector level. The challenge is due in part to the fact that even a project committed to research *in* educational practice needs time to generate insights and understandings. It was therefore only towards the end of the project that we were able to engage in research-informed discussions with tutors, managers and policy-makers. But the difficulty of impact is intensified because the audit culture of Further Education means that colleges have to spend a considerable amount of their time and effort on detailed measures used for funding and inspection. This means, in turn, that the more complex insights of our research are difficult for colleges to 'hear', to acknowledge and incorporate. The cultural approach we have taken and developed has not generated (and cannot generate) simple rules for action or recipes for effective teaching. In our view, the road towards improvement in teaching and learning in Further Education requires that we transform existing learning cultures. This is a process that takes time. It also requires a detailed understanding of how learning cultures work, how they are formed and change over time, how they make learning possible, and how they can be transformed and changed for the better. In the chapters that follow we hope to contribute to the development of such an understanding of learning cultures in Further Education.

Chapter 2

Learning cultures and a cultural theory of learning

Introduction

The notion of 'culture' played a central role in the TLC project. As we have seen in Chapter 1, one of the main purposes of our research was to understand the formation and transformation of learning cultures in FE and the ways in which particular learning cultures create particular learning opportunities. The reason for a focus on learning cultures rather than on teaching or curriculum or student approaches to learning partly followed from our wish to understand teaching and learning in FE in its full complexity. Our assumption at the outset of the project was that learning would depend upon the complex interactions between a range of different factors, aspects and dimensions, rather than on only one or a few of them. We used the notion of 'learning culture' first of all to refer to the particular ways in which the interactions between many different factors shape students' learning opportunities and practices. Learning cultures were, however, not only the object of our research. The idea of a learning culture also crucially shaped our thinking about teaching and learning and improvement. Thus, the TLC project was informed not only by *a theory of learning cultures*, but also by *a cultural theory of learning*, a theory which conceives of learning not as something that happens in the heads, minds or brains of students, but sees it as something that happens in and 'through' social practices. Taken together, the theory of learning cultures and the cultural theory of learning do not only help us to understand the dynamics and complexities of teaching and learning in a different and more 'authentic' way. They also suggest a different approach towards the improvement of teaching and learning, one which focuses on changing the culture

Authored by Phil Hodkinson, Gert Biesta and David James

rather than on only one element of it. It is important for our approach not to forget that the dispositions, actions and individual histories of students are part of the learning culture. This means that student learning is not simply the 'outcome' or 'product' of a particular learning culture but at the very same time also something that shapes the culture. This is one important reason why the idea of 'a science of teaching' – the idea that through research we might be able to find a secure cause–effect relationship between teaching and learning – is simply implausible.

In this chapter we present the main theoretical components of the framework that we have used in the TLC project and that has informed our thinking about the improvement of teaching and learning in FE. We begin with an exploration of the notion of culture in a cultural approach to teaching and learning. We then zoom in on the idea of a learning culture, after which we present our cultural theory of learning. In the final section of this chapter we point at some of the important implications of our approach and indicate how it has informed the research in the TLC project.

The notion of 'culture' in a cultural approach to teaching and learning

To make learning cultures an object of study and to put forward a cultural theory of learning first of all requires clarification of the notion of 'culture' – 'one of the two or three most difficult words in the English language' (Williams 1983: 87). Williams suggests three broad definitions. These are culture as 'a general process of intellectual, spiritual and aesthetic development', culture as 'a particular way of life, whether of a people, a period or a group', and culture as 'the works and practices of intellectual and especially artistic activity' (Williams 1983: 90). Our approach comes closest to the second, anthropological definition of *culture as a way of life*. We see cultures as being constituted – that is, produced and reproduced – by human activity, often but not exclusively, collective activity. To think of culture as human practice does not necessarily entail an agency-driven view of culture, that is, a view which reduces culture to the intentions and actions of individual agents. As we discuss in more detail later, Bourdieu's notions of *field* and *habitus* are meant to overcome the 'either-or' of subjectivist (agency) and objectivist (structure) readings of culture. What our approach does suggest is that cultures exist in and through interaction and communication (Carey 1992; Biesta 1994, 1995, 2004c).

From this it follows that a learning culture is not the same as a learning site. Rather, it is a particular way to understand a learning site as a practice constituted by the actions, dispositions and interpretations of the participants. This is not a one-way process. Cultures are (re)produced by individuals, just as much as individuals are (re)produced by cultures, though individuals are differently positioned with regard to shaping and changing a culture – in other words, differences in power are always at issue too. Cultures, then, are both structured and structuring, and individuals' actions are neither totally determined by the confines of a learning culture, nor are they totally free. A key question that a cultural approach to learning brings to the fore is that of the interplay between 'constraints' and 'affordances' in a learning culture (Wertsch 1998: 45).

One of the most important implications of our understanding of culture is that a learning culture should not be understood as the context or environment within which learning takes place. Rather, 'learning culture' stands for *the social practices through which people learn*. A cultural understanding of learning implies, in other words, that learning is not simply occurring *in* a cultural context, but is itself to be understood *as* a cultural practice. In this we agree with Lave and Wenger (1991: 35) when they state that 'learning is not merely situated in practice – as if it were some independently reifiable process that just happened to be located somewhere; learning is an integral part of generative social practice in the lived-in world.'

Our claim that cultures are constituted by actions, dispositions and interpretations and exist in and through interaction and communication does not mean that learning cultures are invented 'on the spot' or that they can be reinvented at will. Cultures have history and endurance. Artefacts and institutions not only are expressions of cultural practices, but also embody such practices and thus play an important role in the continuation of cultures. For example, the equipment in a language lab or an IT room physically represents a particular pedagogy, as do the organisation of a classroom or a lecture theatre and even the architecture of a college building or site. Without artefacts and a particular physical environment it would be much more difficult to sustain a particular learning culture. Artefacts and institutions cannot play their role by themselves. They need to be used and enacted in order to exert their influence, much as Wenger (1998) illustrates with reference to reification and participation (see also Biesta 2004c). But the meaning of artefacts and institutions is not completely malleable. Actors always operate within systems of expectations: the expectations they bring to the situation and the expectations that others have about their activities and practices. Teachers engage with their tasks on the basis of ideas about what it means to be a teacher, just as students do not come to college as *tabulae rasae* but with ideas about what 'appropriate' student behaviour consists of. Similarly, governments, policy-makers, employers, administrators, funding agencies and 'the public' have ideas and expectations about the educational system in general, and FE in particular. Such expectations influence, structure and limit what is possible for those working inside the system. The key issue here is not simply *that* there are different expectations, but that some of them are more influential than others, reflecting fundamental differences in power. Some change is possible but it often happens slowly. Furthermore, expectations are not necessarily consciously held. Many expectations exist at the level of dispositions (see below). They exist as 'ways of doing' and 'ways of being' that are considered to be 'normal'.

If, as we contend, learning cultures should be understood as the practices through which people – students and tutors – learn, then it follows that the key task for a cultural approach to learning is to understand how particular practices impact upon the learning opportunities of the participants. The central question is what forms and ways of learning are made possible within a particular learning culture, and what forms of learning are made difficult or sometimes even impossible. To answer this question we need, on the one hand, an understanding of the dynamics of learning cultures and how they 'work'. We need to understand how particular learning cultures come into existence, how they stay in existence, how they change over time – both as a result of deliberate attempts and as the result of intervening events and unintended consequences of actions – and how learning cultures decline and eventually disappear. To do so we need a theory of learning cultures that is able to operate across the different scales through which learning can be understood. On the other hand we need an understanding of the ways in which learning happens through participation in a learning culture. We need, in other words, a cultural theory of learning which understands learning in practical terms, as something that is done, and hence as something that is embodied, not simply cognitive, that is socially situated, not simply located in the individual, and that understands learning as entailing agentic action and structural characteristics. In the following two sections we introduce our theory of learning cultures and our cultural theory of learning.

A theory of learning cultures

In the TLC project our prime focus was on the practices of learning and teaching within the nineteen sites. In this respect our approach was in keeping with many other studies of learning as participation, which tend to focus on the specifics of a localised setting. Despite the considerable diversity of sites (some were classrooms, some combined classrooms and workplaces, some were individuals in scattered workplaces, others were virtual, being an internet connection between tutor and students), the idea of a learning site has high resonance with conventional notions of how learning is 'bounded', or located. In all cases, the site was drawn at a fairly large scale, as it had to be, if the detailed ways in which learning took place were to be understood. However, the boundaries of the learning cultures identified within the sites could not be so easily drawn. Among the factors that potentially impact upon a particular learning site and constitute the learning culture, there are many that operate and largely originate from outside the site itself. Put differently: while learning sites can have relatively clear boundaries, the factors that constitute the learning culture in a particular site do not. They spread well beyond it. One way to grapple more effectively with this issue is through Bourdieu's concept of *field*.

The most useful analogies for understanding Bourdieu's notion of field are those of 'market' and 'game', though both can be misleading if pressed too hard. A field is like a *market* because it is a defined social space in which there is inequality but also mutual dependency. Individual customers differ in how much purchasing power they have, by virtue of having different characteristics, backgrounds and tastes. 'Purchasing power' may take the conventional form of economic capital, but can just as much mean social capital (for example, who you know and who knows you) or cultural capital (for example, knowing the deeper and often less obvious ways in which the field works). The notion of *game* draws attention to the idea that people are in competition for the maintenance or increase of capital of one sort or another, and over the rules of the game. These 'rules' are both written and unwritten, denoting a general agreement in the expectations and presuppositions of the contestants. They can and do change. There are also alliances and more or less permanent cooperative agreements within the larger competition. Moreover, as in a game, the field is in flux (there is something to 'play for') rather than presenting a set of foregone conclusions, and the parties 'believe in the game they are playing and in the value of what is at stake in the struggles they are waging' (Vandenberghe

2000: 399). However, this is not the same thing as seeing the game for what it is, and this is where the analogy breaks down. Lots of social practices appear as one thing while achieving something else, with the people involved not necessarily seeing how this works. Bourdieu's term for this is *misrecognition*. For Bourdieu, a parent's decision to place their child in the 'best' school to which they will pay high fees is often framed as an educational decision, that is, as the 'best' education for their child. This can mask an underlying interest which may be summed up as an attempt to convert economic into cultural capital in order to maintain or enhance their social position. In the learning sites we studied, there were several social practices that meant one thing to the immediate participants while appearing rather differently if analysed with the theoretical tools we brought to bear (Colley et al. 2003b).

Bourdieu's notion of *field* was most developed via his work about art, where he wrote that a field is a 'configuration of relations between positions objectively defined, in their existence and in the determinations they impose upon the occupants, agents or institutions' (Bourdieu 1992: 72–73). Grenfell and James (2004) note that the medium of these relations and determinations is some form of *capital*, that *time* operates in several different ways through a field, and that fields can be more or less *autonomous* – that is, fields vary in how much they depend on other fields to define them. However, all fields are related to some extent to the field of power. It is also worth noting that in most of the examples one can read in Bourdieu's own work, *field* refers to large entities mapped out using a small scale (as in 'the field of education', or 'cultural production', 'art', or 'fashion'). In the TLC project we use field to assist in analysis at several scales, including the individual, local and institutional. We see *field* as a conceptual tool for understanding learning cultures. Indeed, Bourdieu's tools are all devices for getting a grip on culture in the way we have defined it.

If we focus on English FE for the purposes of illustration, then colleges and the learning sites are positioned within the field of English FE, as are a long list of quasi-autonomous government organisations and many individuals and groups of individuals, including students and tutors. The learning cultures in the sites we studied were, then, part of a wider learning culture, influenced by what can usefully be seen as several overlapping fields. Those wider fields operated beyond the site and also within it, so that though the site could be bounded, the learning culture could not. Field dynamics impact differently from site to site, and some struggles that were highly important in site A were hardly present in site B. Not only were the internal dynamics of sites different, so too were their positions, relative to each other and to these wider fields. Consequently, to understand the learning culture of any one site, it was necessary to understand the field of FE as a whole, and the relationship of the site to that field, and to other fields of which it was part or with which it interacted. This latter point can be seen most clearly in the vocational sites, which were also part of the employment fields that they targeted. Sometimes a vocational site had very close links with particular types of employers. This was the case in a nursery nursing course and the result was not only highly effective learning related to doing the job, but also severe restrictions on the extent to which tutors could challenge or even question the existing practices in that field. In an electronic engineering course, specific employer demands led to a highly responsive course restructuring, converting a two-year programme into a one-year version. However, this was in the context of a longer-term process of decline, linked to fundamental shifts in the industry, such as changes in the nature of its products and changes in international location of manufacturing. These changes reinforced a continuing lack of synergy between course content and workplace need, and a lack of student-perceived relevance of the course. By contrast, one business studies course was almost completely detached from the employment field it claimed to serve. This made job progression and the integration of learning with actual occupational practices very difficult. These examples show how the concept of field assists us in describing the processes and practices within each site, and how these contributed to the construction the learning culture.

The fields operating in the sites and FE are related to wide social and economic pressures. Bourdieu wrote about the field of power, which interpenetrates all others. This is the field of macro-political social relations, and of power broking by major multinational corporations and the media, among others. Put another way, FE and the colleges and sites within it are interpenetrated by issues of social class, gender and ethnicity, and issues of globalisation that cut across society as a whole. This interpenetration across scales is a major reason why it is a mistake to think of a learning culture or field as having precise boundaries. But it also helps us to understand how some changes in FE, driven by the wider field of power (and by economic imperatives in particular), can make individual tutors feel that they are being placed – or choose to place themselves – 'beyond the bounds' of FE colleges' 'cost-effectiveness' measures for the viability of learning sites in response to changes in the FE funding regime, or the government's reduction of funding for asylum seekers wishing to learn English, for example, can mean that the possibilities for tutors to pursue their own professional practice and values become difficult to sustain in new circumstances (see examples of this in Chapters 4 and 6).

In this way, any learning culture functions and is constructed and reconstructed through the forces of one or more fields. Seeing fields as primarily concerned with forces, as having imprecise and overlapping boundaries, and as existing at all scales, overcomes several of the weaknesses in existing participatory views of learning. It locates power relations at the heart of understanding learning. It can operationalise the links between learning cultures and wider social structures, while retaining the possibility of a large scale focus on localised learning sites, where, as Lave (1996: 161–162) correctly argues '(t)here are enormous differences in what and how learners come to shape (or be shaped into) their identities with respect to different practices. . . . Researchers would have to explore each practice to understand what is being learned, and how.' For us, the key issue is how different learning cultures enable or disable different possibilities for the people that come into contact with them. The notion of field acts as a constant reminder that a course or an institution is not just a place or a context for learning, but is *positioned* in relation to others. This in turn means that a learning culture will permit, promote, inhibit or rule out certain kinds of learning.

The key aspects of our theory of learning cultures

- Learning cultures are not the contexts in which people learn, but the social practices through which people learn.
- This means that individuals influence and are part of learning cultures just as learning cultures influence and are part of individuals.
- Learning cultures are not the same as learning sites. While learning sites have clear boundaries, the factors that constitute the learning culture(s) in a particular site do not.
- We use Bourdieu's notions of *field* and *habitus* as conceptual tools for understanding learning cultures.
- Any learning culture functions and is constructed and reconstructed through the forces of one or more fields.
- A learning culture will permit, promote, inhibit or rule out certain kinds of learning. This means that the key issue is how different learning cultures enable or disable different learning possibilities for the people that come into contact with them.

A cultural theory of learning

Thus far we have focused on understanding learning cultures and how the notion of field assists in that. We now need to consider how individuals learn through participation in learning cultures, which brings us to the cultural theory of learning that we have used in the TLC project. Given that we see learning cultures as the social practices through which people learn, our cultural theory of learning starts from the assumption that learning is something that is *done* – which for us means that learning has to be understood as practical and embodied, and not simply as mental – and that it is *done with others* – which means that learning has to be understood as a thoroughly social process. Although social practices are the result of social action and interaction, such practices are not simply the outcome of individual actions but also of wider structural factors. One of the challenges for a cultural theory of learning is therefore also to account for the complex interplay between structure and agency. We unfold our approach to understanding learning in three steps. We first look at the way in which we understand the dynamic interplay between individual and culture. We then discuss what we mean by the idea that learning is practical and embodied, after which we explore the social dimension of learning and the learner.

Placing individual learners in the learning culture

In attempting to integrate an individual learner with the learning culture through which s/he learns, we face a linguistic and textual problem. In a linear script we have to start with one or the other: the individual or the learning culture. Whatever way round this is done, the result is a distortion of the relational reality. Thus, in approaching the learning culture of a site as part of one or more fields, we must not make a classical error of assuming that this sums up everything about the individuals whom we see, relationally, within that culture. Though a learning culture *may* be highly immersing and intensively defining in relation to a student within it, this should not prevent us from seeing 'the person behind the student', which is another way of saying that the individual will always be part of other fields too. Similarly, as we have argued, it is a mistake to see the learning culture of a site as the external context within which the individual acts and learns. Individuals influence and are part of learning cultures just as learning cultures influence and are part of individuals.

Each participant in a learning culture contributes to the construction and reconstruction of that culture. Bourdieu provides us with several conceptual tools for understanding the complexity of this interrelationship. The impact of an individual on a learning culture depends upon a combination of their position within that culture, their dispositions towards that culture, and the various types of capital (social, cultural and economic) that they possess. Participants can influence the nature of the field and the learning culture within which they participate intentionally, through striving to change and/or preserve certain characteristics or practices. For the tutors in our sites, this sort of deliberate intervention was part of their job, but students sometimes worked on the culture intentionally also. However, much of the impact of individuals in a learning culture is the result of their presence and actions within it, whether they intend to influence that culture or not. Thus, the very presence of young working-class women reinforced key parts of the learning culture in the nursery nursing site. In a distance learning for basic IT skills site, the diverse nature of the students, their desire to learn at home without face-to-face contact, and the ways in which they and the tutors interacted through telephone and emails were integral parts of a distinctive set of practices that made up the learning culture. Expressed differently, a field operates at the scale of individual interactions, as well as the more macro-scales that Bourdieu was primarily concerned with.

Learning as practical, embodied and social

Long before the current wave of socio-cultural theories of learning, John Dewey (1859–1952) had argued that learning is thoroughly practical and involves not simply the human mind but the living human being in continuous interaction with its environment (Dewey 1957, 1990; see also Biesta 1994, 1995). Dewey challenged the idea that mind and body are separate, with the mind being the true location of human cognition and learning, and with mental/rational processes as being superior to the emotional and the practical. For Dewey mind is not a separate entity but a function of intelligent human action, action that is characterised by anticipation, foresight, and embodied judgement (see Dewey 1963). Challenges to this mind–body dualism have also been central to feminist perspectives on learning and the formation of identity, on which we have also drawn. For example, Hochschild's (1983) seminal work on emotional labour, drawing on a Marxist feminist analysis, and subsequent development of this topic (for example, Bates 1990, 1991, 1994; Colley 2003), foregrounds the deeply embodied, classed-gendered practices associated with learning to practise the management of feeling, illuminating a whole sphere of analysis for our project.

The practical and embodied nature of college learning is clearly shown in our data. All college courses directly involve the practical and emotional as well as the mental. In the nursery nursing course, where mainly young women are trained as nursery workers, the emphasis was mainly on how to do the job, which was learned through a combination of doing it (both on placement and in college activities) and by thinking about what the work did and/or should entail, in discussions, group work and workshops. In both, there was considerable focus on how to do and how to be, with a strong sense of *vocational becoming* (Colley et al. 2003b). In all sites, there was a practical and emotional engagement with the learning as an activity that students participated in. Practical engagement might entail sitting at desks, writing notes, asking or answering questions and listening to the teacher (for example in AS Psychology), as well as more obviously practical actions, such as editing a photographic image or speaking in a foreign language, as in some other sites. Even in classes like psychology, the embodied nature of what goes on can be seen, for example in the ways people sit, move and interact, in the ways they use books, computers and pens. The emotional is readily apparent. As well as indications of joy, boredom, frustration or anger, in many sites there were deeper engagements. Thus, nursery nurse students were subconsciously learning that emotional labour – a selfless giving of themselves while repressing their personal feelings – was required in the job (Colley 2006). Entry Level Drama students were active in constructing their course as a second family – a place where they felt comfortable, and where tutors were pressured to adopt parenting roles. Engineering students, too, had to do substantial work on their feelings, to cope with the demands of studying on top of doing a full-time job with day release, and to endure in the face of frustration with the perceived irrelevance of their studies to their learning on the job (Colley et al. 2003b). In sum, college-based learning is embodied, from the most 'practical' through to the most 'academic' courses.

The learning of the individual is also social. This is another key idea in the work of pragmatists like John Dewey and George Herbert Mead (1863–1931). It is especially Mead who shows that the social is not 'outside' the individual but exists in and through interaction, participation and communication (see Biesta 1999), while Smith takes this a step further to point to the ways in which language itself 'already has a determinate capacity to mean' (Smith 1999: 111) before it is activated in social interactions. This parallels Bourdieu's insistence that 'the preconstructed' is everywhere, and 'does not necessarily contain within itself the principles of its own interpretation' (Bourdieu and Wacquant 1992: 74). Furthermore, as Bourdieu points out, people are always socially positioned. Though he concentrates on social class, the argument equally applies to issues of gender and ethnicity, of nationality or local community. While this can be seen as part of social identity, Bourdieu prefers the term *habitus*. He defines habitus as a battery of 'durable, transposable' dispositions to all aspects of life that are often subconscious or tacit. They develop from our social positions, and through our lives. The habitus can also be seen as social structures operating within and through individuals, rather than something outside of us. Just as mind and body are not separated, neither are the individual and social structures. Bloomer and Hodkinson (2002) show how students as social individuals act upon the learning opportunities they encounter. In Bloomer's (1997) terminology, they construct their learning through studentship, and are not passive recipients of what tutors (or the system) tries to do to them. But their studentship cannot be separated out from the social structures that interpenetrate their habitus, and the differing types and amounts of cultural capital they possess. Also, life outside college can have a major impact on college learning. The social and embodied student cannot insulate their college learning and other parts of their lives, even if he or she chooses to see them as separate.

Another way of understanding the significance of habitus for individual learning is that students have a significant existence prior to entering a learning site. It is through these prior experiences that the dispositions that make up the habitus were developed. These largely tacit dispositions orientate people in relation to anything they do in life, including learning. These pre-existing orientations helped explain similarities and differences in learning, within and between TLC sites. In the AS Psychology site the part-time adult students were there with very different dispositions towards the course. Some wanted to pass the examination in order to advance their careers, others had a general interest. The dispositions of some included prior understandings and attitudes towards academic work, others did not. Some appeared disposed to work hard, while others were waiting for the tutor to engage their interest, or even just passing the time. In the nursery nursing site, there was a much more homogeneous grouping of young working-class white women, most of whom were already committed to working in this area. However, even here, differences in disposition were important. One older student talked of the ways in which the course was challenging her existing practices as a single parent, suggesting that many of the things she did with her own child were inappropriate. Thus, a person's dispositions enable some forms of learning, while constraining or preventing others.

Such dispositions amount to more than attitudes, motivations and interests. They also include ways of dressing and behaving and ways of performing. A group of less able young people, on an Entry Level Drama course, proved adept in making their tutors act as surrogate parents, solving even small problems for them. They did this through their collective embodied actions. The result was that their learning further reinforced their sense of dependency, even as they hoped for greater independence and autonomy.

We should understand these dispositions as having developed through a student's past life. They are a product of accumulated lived experience – in home, school, work, leisure and in local communities. Thus, the concept of habitus, with its constituent dispositions, directly links the social nature of the person with their ongoing social and embodied learning. Within the educational experiences that were the subject of our research, student dispositions were further developed, and also could be further developed in the other parts of a student's life, that ran parallel with and possibly overlapped their college participation. Sometimes, existing dispositions were reinforced. Sometimes, new dispositions could be formed, or existing dispositions modified and changed. One way of understanding learning, therefore, is as a process through which a person's dispositions are confirmed, developed, challenged or changed.

The concept of habitus expresses the sense in which the individual is social. A person's dispositions are never completely unique, but share characteristics with others sharing similar social positions, backgrounds and experiences. However, because everyone's life experience is partly unique, habitus as a concept is neither deterministic nor totalising. Within a cultural view of learning, habitus helps us to keep in view the individual *and* social nature of a person's learning and teaching. In doing so, it aids the integration of a cultural theory of learning, within a theory of learning cultures.

Bourdieu's notion of habitus thus helps to understand the extent to which learning happens as a result of our embodied engagement in cultural practices. It is important to see, however, that learning is more than the subconscious transformation of our dispositions. We learn not only by doing but also by reflecting upon what we do and by consciously monitoring our actions. Tennis players do not acquire their habitus and feel for the game without some conscious monitoring of their actions. They need motivation and concentration not only to get their skills 'right' but also to understand 'the point' of the game of tennis. According to Bourdieu, therefore, habitus not only generates meaningful practices, but also generates 'meaning-giving perceptions' (Bourdieu 1984: 170, quoted in Sayer 2005: 27). As Sayer explains: 'Ways of thinking can become habitual. Once learned they change from something we struggle to grasp to something we can think *with*.' It is therefore important not to reduce the formation of habitus to mere conditioning because 'some dispositions are based on understanding' (Sayer 2005: 28). The difference between learning by emulation and understanding is that in the latter case 'one grasps reasons and rationales' (Sayer 2005: 28); one sees, in other words, 'the point' of doing something in a particular way.

Key aspects of our cultural theory of learning

- A cultural theory of learning aims to understand how individuals learn through their participation in learning cultures.
- The relationship between individuals and learning cultures is reciprocal: individuals influence and are part of learning cultures just as learning cultures influence and are part of individuals.
- The impact of an individual on a learning culture depends upon a combination of their position within that culture, their dispositions towards that culture, and the various types of capital (social, cultural and economic) that they possess. Much of their impact is the result of their presence and actions within it, whether they intend to influence that culture or not.
- Learning has to be understood as something that is done, which means that it has to be understood as practical and embodied and not simply as occurring in the mind.
- Thus, learning has to be understood as something that is done with others, which means that it has to be understood as a thoroughly social process.
- To understand the social dimensions of learning and the learner we use Bourdieu's notions of *habitus* and *field*. Habitus stands for a battery of durable, transposable dispositions to all aspects of life that are often subconscious or tacit. They develop from our

social positions with the field and can be seen as social structures operating within and through individuals.

- Learning can be seen as a process through which a person's dispositions are confirmed, developed, challenged or changed.
- Although much learning takes place through the subconscious (trans)formation of dispositions, some of our learning requires conscious effort and attention and reflection in order to understand the 'point' of particular actions, activities and (cultural) practices.

Conclusion

In this chapter we have outlined the theoretical approach which has informed the TLC project. This approach consists of two interlocking parts: a theory of learning cultures and a cultural theory of learning. There is a reciprocal relationship between the two parts. Whereas a cultural theory of learning aims to understand how people learn through their participation in learning cultures, we see learning cultures themselves as the practices through which people learn. The central question in our approach is therefore also a double one. On the one hand the question is how a particular learning culture will permit, promote, inhibit or rule out certain kinds of learning. On the other hand we ask how people learn through their engagement with particular learning cultures. We have introduced the notions of field and habitus as tools to better understand the workings of learning cultures and to better understand the learning practices within particular cultures.

One important benefit of the cultural approach taken in the TLC project is that it provides us with a much more holistic way of looking at learners, learning and their learning practices. Within the FE sector at the time of our research, particular measurable outcomes – the achievement of qualifications and student retention rates – were seen as the predominant purpose of learning, outcomes which were also accepted as reliable measures of the effectiveness of learning. Thus, learning was successful if students stayed until the end, and then passed the formal assessments. While achieving a qualification is without doubt important for individuals, we would not be able to understand the complexities of learning if we would only focus on this and forget about the wider picture. Seeing the wider picture is precisely what the cultural approach helped us to do. It helped us to see, for example, that being a student in FE does not simply result in the acquisition of knowledge and skills and a qualification, but that it affects the whole person. The reason for this is that in some way or another it is always the whole person who learns and who changes as a result of the learning. The cultural approach helps us to see that learning can change aspects of people's habitus, it can change and/or reinforce what they know, what they can do, how they see themselves, who they are. That is, through learning, people come to be someone, or to be someone else. In becoming, there will be significant differences, as well as similarities, between students who participate in the same learning culture. The outcomes of a college course are based partly on what was learned before the student enrolled, may be partly based on experiences outside the course, and may continue after the course has been completed. There are often many outcomes before the course is completed, and the lack of a qualification does not mean that significant outcomes are absent.

The cultural approach thus also helps us to understand in much more detail the role of values and normative orientations at play in FE. Looking at learning in a more holistic way allows us to ask important questions about the purposes of FE, or of a particular course, or about learning in any other context. It draws our attention to fundamental questions about the education of the whole person rather than the acquisition of a particular set of skills. Thus, we might argue for a skilled plumber as a person who understands and can think historically, a person with a rounded education, a person with compassion and a sense of democratic responsibility. The question about which of these is desirable entails contestable and often contested value judgements. If learning is culturally constructed, so is the view about what counts as good learning. Because such judgements are contestable, it is likely that different students, different tutors, different college managers, employers, parents, and policy-makers, will have differing views about the outcomes that are desired, and our research evidence confirms that – and such views and the struggle over the definition of what counts as good or desirable learning are themselves important constituents of learning cultures too. Also, whatever the intentions and whatever the planning, there will always be unintended outcomes, and outcomes will differ from student to student.

The cultural approach also enables us to adopt a different and in our opinion more realistic way to understand and manage the improvement of teaching and learning. The essence of this approach is to work to enhance learning cultures, in ways that make successful learning more rather than less likely. Because of the relational complexity of learning, and of the differing positions and dispositions of learners, there is no approach that can ever guarantee universal learning success, however success is defined. Rather than looking for universal solutions that will work always, everywhere, and for everyone, the cultural approach helps us to see that the improvement of learning cultures always asks for contextualised judgement rather than for general recipes.

Part II

What does the research tell us?

In Part II of the book we show how the cultural approach has helped us to ask new questions about teaching and learning in FE and, as a result of this, has generated new and important insights about teaching and learning in FE. We have organised the presentation and discussion of our findings in response to three questions which follow directly from the theoretical framework outlined in Chapter 1. In Chapters 3 and 4 we ask 'What are learning cultures in FE and how do they change?'. As we have argued, particularly through the notion of 'field', learning cultures are not the same as learning sites, particular courses or particular classroom practices. Learning cultures have many different manifestations and can exist at many different levels. In Chapter 3 we therefore attempt to characterise the learning culture(s) of the FE sector and how it has developed over the past decades. In Chapter 4 we focus on the learning cultures of the particular sites we investigated in the TLC project. If learning cultures are the practices through which people learn, then one of the important questions is 'How do learning cultures transform people?'. This is the guiding question for Chapter 5, in which we first of all focus on the particular practices of learning that we found in our sites. We then turn this idea on its head and focus on one important aspect of our findings, namely, the fact that students in FE do not simply acquire knowledge and skills and qualifications, but actually learn practices. In Chapters 6 and 7 we ask 'How can learning cultures be improved?'. As we have said before, the main implication from our cultural approach is that in order to improve teaching and learning we should improve learning cultures. In Chapters 6 and 7 we ask how people – the different actors in FE – can change and transform learning cultures. In Chapter 6 we explore in more detail how this can be done and how we should understand the ways in which people can deliberately try to change learning cultures, given that learning cultures are complex social practices. In Chapter 7 we zoom out again and ask wider questions about the role and position of educational professionals in learning cultures.

Chapter 3

Improving teaching and learning in FE
A policy history

Introduction

In Chapter 2 we argued that a *learning culture* is a way in which a *learning site* can be understood, as the social practices through which people learn. We also said that the elements of a learning culture are not invented, as it were, on the spot, but have enduring features: some of the more obvious ones would be buildings, physical spaces and textbooks, but there are many other equally important elements that are harder to see, such as sets of expectations about what kinds of learning are held to be worthwhile.

Our starting point is the metaphor of map-making: most people are accustomed to seeing maps of different kinds which represent a complex physical world in different ways, for different purposes. Maps are also drawn to a particular scale. While later chapters adopt a large scale, and 'zoom in' to look up close and in detail at various learning sites and their cultural features, in this chapter we 'zoom out' to a smaller scale, in order to illustrate what the TLC project found to be important about the generic learning culture of the FE sector. In this respect, the metaphor is not just a spatial one, but also temporal – maps of the same place in different eras help to identify those features that have changed and those that remain the same. We felt it was important to take a long view of the history of FE, and in particular of repeated calls for its improvement throughout that history, in order to contextualise our own study. All too often, practitioners are overwhelmed by 'initiative fatigue' induced by the latest episode of 'policy hysteria' (Stronach and Morris 1994) proclaiming that teaching and learning need improving. By adopting a longer-term mapping of these calls for improvement, we can

Authored by Helen Colley, Madeleine Wahlberg and David James

begin to learn something important about what notions of improvement have been prevalent, why they have been so oft repeated, and some key aspects of continuity and change in the sector.

With some difficulty (since much of the documentary material we were looking for has been destroyed each time that FE or its national bodies have been restructured), we traced and reviewed around 300 texts written since the Second World War, all concerned with the improvement of teaching and learning in FE: academic texts, research reports, teacher training and development materials, and policy documents. We were able to locate the most significant (though still partial) archive of reports from the Further Education Unit (FEU), which advised colleges and local education authorities (LEAs) on curriculum management and practice in the light of government policy for Further Education and training from 1977, and from the Further Education Development Agency, which replaced the FEU in 1995, and has itself been succeeded by the Learning and Skills Development Agency in 2000 and the Quality Improvement Agency in 2005. While so many of these documents suggested that teaching and learning in FE needed improvement, we were principally struck by how few of them discussed teaching and learning in any detail. Pedagogy and learning theory were, for the most part, singularly invisible. It is this paradox that we explore as a central issue for the history of FE in this chapter.

The chapter begins with a look at the way that teaching and learning are often positioned in writing about FE, and notes this silence around them in such policy documents and discourses. We turn to both official documents and project data to sketch some of the main themes in the various 'stories of improvement' we identified in the sector. Finally, we select a critical moment in the recent history of the sector when teaching and learning did gain direct and explicit attention, and contrast it with current policy prescriptions for 14–19 education, in order to illustrate a pattern in how teaching and learning figure in either the 'diagnosis' or the 'remedy' for improving FE.

Teaching and learning in FE: what goes without saying?

There are a number of well-researched historical studies which have charted structural, political and institutional changes in English FE, from its earliest origins in the craft guilds, 'whisky money' and the mechanics institutes,[1] through to industrial, professional and local education authority control and, more recently, to the rise of the Manpower

Services Commission (MSC) and (in 1992) Incorporation (see for example, Avis et al. 1996; Ainley and Bailey 1997; Green and Lucas 1999; Hyland and Merrill 2003; Stanton and Bailey 2004).[2] Such histories are essential to understanding the state – and status – of FE in England today. However, it is rare for them to address practices of teaching and learning directly, because their main purposes are, rightly, elsewhere.

A different type of text is aimed at helping prepare people to teach in the sector, and this might be expected to engage more directly with those practices. However, whether informed by psychological or sociological perspectives, this writing has tended to isolate practices to do with teaching and learning from their context. L.B. Curzon's popular work, now in its sixth edition, is a good example: 'Problems related to difficulties in retrieving and reinstating learned information are fundamentally the same for students in Bolton, Berlin or Bejing' (Curzon 2004: 21). Curzon recognises the effect of what he calls the 'cultural and social overlay' on this, but the point is that a *learning process* is kept separate from a discrete notion of *culture*, with the latter amounting to a context or container in which learning takes place. A different sort of text advocates that would-be teachers should adopt one of three main value-systems that will give them a fundamental pedagogy, which they can then apply to differing social and policy contexts (Armitage et al. 1999). Yet even insightful and thought-provoking discussions about the context itself – about such matters as organisation, managerialism, vocationalism and accountability in post-compulsory education – can be conducted in a language that keeps them detached from teaching and learning practices (see, for example, Lea et al. 2003).

As was described in Chapters 1 and 2, both the design and the theoretical roots of the TLC project gave the team a constant encouragement to try to overcome the classic separation of practice and context. There were a few helpful examples already, such as Ainley and Bailey's (1997) interpretation of pedagogy as the mediation of political pressures on FE. The Further Education Unit's (1992) *Quality Education and Training for the Adult Unemployed: A manual for planners and managers in FE* is an interesting, if less consciously critical, example which traced how the pedagogy of 'student centred learning' was originally developed for a 'dysfunctional' group of learners by practitioners with a radical agenda. It goes on to show how, when the Manpower Services Commission inherited responsibility for this 'dysfunctional' group in 1981, it set about denaturing the pedagogy so that it was retained in form, but not in content. However, such examples did not add up to a history of pedagogy in FE, nor an overview of the generation or emergence of a problem called 'the need to improve teaching and learning in FE'. Since the TLRP, and therefore the TLC project within it, was required to ask 'how teaching and learning could be improved', in order to answer the question productively, we realised that we first had to turn the question on itself:

- Why has improving teaching and learning in FE been construed as a 'problem'? By whom? And in whose interests?
- How has that problem been constructed, and how has its meaning endured, been contested, or changed over time?
- What prefigured notions of 'best practice' have been constructed by colleges, practitioners, agencies, inspection bodies, employers and government over time? And with what outcomes?
- What key developments in policy, pedagogy and practice in FE have intervened to restrict or transform its course?

These are big and important questions. While we cannot hope to give very full answers to them in the space available here, we would suggest that there are many serious ramifications to ignoring them. Coffield (2000) has remarked before on a silence around this issue, and its practical importance:

> In all the plans to put learners first, to invest in learning, to widen participation, to set targets, to develop skills, to open access, to raise standards, and to develop a national framework of qualifi-cations, there is no mention of a theory (or theories) of learning to drive the whole project. It is as though there existed in the UK such a widespread understanding of, and agreement about, the processes of learning and teaching that comment was thought superfluous. The omission is serious and, if not corrected, could prove fatal to the enterprise.
>
> (Coffield 2000: 18)

The lack of clear and shared ideas about learning was a constant source of frustration for tutors who participated in the TLC project, as the following typical comments show:

> We won't be able to improve teaching and learning until there is continuity in the college. The constant changes in staffing, courses and policy get in the way of good teaching. Restless colleges, like

a form of institutional ADHD [attention deficit hyperactivity disorder], do not make good learners.

What hinders good teaching and learning is that the college is designed around the delivery of easy management and profits. We need a fundamentally different architecture – based on the actual process of teaching and learning.

These views underline other data we have which suggests a paucity of conversations (and indeed developmental opportunities) concerned with teaching and learning in many FE colleges, accompanied by constant change and by a highly managed environment. However, this cannot be taken to mean that theories of learning and teaching are simply 'absent'. It is more likely to mean that certain theories are so taken-for-granted and pervasive that they are virtually invisible, or 'go without saying'.

Telling tales of improving FE

In FE before the Second World War, although there was little discussion of teaching and learning, this did not mean an absence of underpinning theory. FE provided the narrow vocational training that employers needed for a relatively privileged fraction of the working class, the white male labour aristocracy in craft occupations. The curriculum was determined centrally by examining boards dominated by employers, and FE had no direct ownership of its curriculum. The role of the teacher was to deliver centrally determined syllabi by means of didactic lectures and demonstrations. In its voluntarism and entrepreneurialism, FE appeared unsystematic, but in fact it can be seen as the very opposite in its responsiveness to employers. In this respect, there was a high synergy between the purposes and the pedagogy: FE did what it said on the tin, and there was no *general* spur to discuss what learning did or could mean (Gleeson and Mardle 1980).

There is broad agreement in academic studies that FE in England has passed through a series of phases since the Second World War, although throughout this time it has been continually plagued by the problem of its voluntaristic nature. Stanton and Bailey (2004) summarise three key periods in its evolution: the thirty years post-war in which a series of attempts to legislate for individual and employer participation in vocational education and training came to little; a brief interlude from the mid-1970s to the mid-1980s, in which curriculum reform through specific delivery arrangements took centre stage, in response to the collapse of the youth labour market and the mass entry of young people into FE; and, since the end of the 1980s, a decisive shift by government to control vocational education and training (VET) through the regulation of qualifications, tied to audit-dominated funding and inspection regimes.

Against this background, we found some remarkable continuities in the references made to improving teaching and learning. In fifty years of literature, there were repeated appeals about the *need* to improve teaching and learning, but very little that addressed *how* this should be done. The Crowther Report (1959) is a prime example. This was a major research-based report, prompted principally by a projected demographic bulge, to advise the government on post-compulsory education. In addressing the question of educational 'failure', it refers to:

> [the] student's age on leaving school, the type of school he [*sic*] has attended, the conditions under which he has taken the course . . . the nature of his home background as shown by his father's occupation, his general vigour as shown by his participation in games, and the difficulty he found in certain subjects in the course.
>
> (Crowther 1959: 362)

The question of how 'he' was taught is not on this agenda. Nor does it appear in the report's analysis of principal defects in FE: the school-to-college transition; insufficient time for apprentices to complete courses; the need for more breadth in course content; and the small proportion of teachers who were full-time (20 per cent) or trained (25 per cent). But Crowther did have things to say about how FE should change in order to address these problems and make improvements to teaching and learning possible. The Crowther Report advocated above all that teaching should become more closely allied to 'other forms of social work'. Teaching and learning have a shadowy presence in the diagnosis, but then become a central part of the remedy.

As we reviewed academic, practitioner-oriented and policy documents alongside our data, we found that this history revealed at least twenty-four different 'stories' about transforming FE which called forth the need to improve teaching and learning. One of the ways in which we looked across these accounts was to tease out how they addressed three things, namely:

- *Drivers* for change: the reasons *why* teaching and learning need to be improved.

- *Levers* for change: the *mechanisms* suggested for spurring improvements to teaching and learning.
- *Pedagogical change* itself: arguments about *how* teaching and learning can or should be improved.

The following sections address each of these in turn.

Drivers for improving teaching and learning

The large majority of texts we looked at were, like the Crowther Report, dominated by discourses about why teaching and learning in FE needed to be improved. These are therefore teleological tales: pedagogy is implicitly dependent on the wider purposes that FE is supposed to serve, and the problem of 'improving teaching and learning' is ritually invoked as the solution to a range of external problems. Three of the major themes that run through these stories relate to youth and social cohesion, employers' needs, and the economics of FE.

The problem of youth and social cohesion

Some texts focus on FE as one of the moral and social responses to the 'problem of youth'. They appeal to issues such as the breakdown of the family; the loss of moral compass in the face of new sexual freedoms; the pending crisis of leisure time; the collapse of the youth labour market; the fear of 'yob' culture (at different times, this centres variously on young men, pregnant teenagers, rebellious black youth, the 'underclass'); the rediscovery of poverty and social inclusion agendas; and the need for what would now be termed emotional literacy. The Crowther Report was a prime example of this, driven by concerns about the family and by the expected increase in leisure time – what would the youth do with so much spare time, and no family discipline? Ethel Venables (1968), writing ten years later, presented a surprisingly similar picture. Her view of the 'problem' of teenagers was that 'they live in the present and largely outside their homes, which provide little comfort other than a roof'. Pedagogy in this 'story' not only was framed as ensuring that this social role for FE would be effective, but also led to criticisms of its role in 'warehousing' people after the collapse of the youth labour market in the 1970s.

The effectiveness of the provision

Others focus instead on issues about the nature of appropriate VET. There are debates about the essence of a 'good apprenticeship'; standards and quality in VET; the introduction of new technology and increased skill demands of work; responses to changes in the labour market, especially the shift from manufacturing to services; demographic change, linked to labour market supply and demand (are there too few or too many young people to meet demand, and are they inadequately skilled); the need for liberal studies, general education or citizenship classes alongside a vocational focus so as to ensure the maintenance of democracy and prevent social anomie. The National Association of Teachers in Further and Higher Education (NATFHE 1983), the main teacher union in FE, attacked the MSC for their lack of clarity about the purpose of FE, arguing that by confusing education with training and pursuing contradictory aims, the MSC would be unable to deliver on its learning agenda. More recently, Unwin (2002) has been critical of both the conditions of the teachers of apprentices, and of the conditions of the workplace for the apprentices themselves. She argues that the conditions of both sets of workers will need to be improved in order to achieve the purposes of apprenticeship learning. The Foster Report (Foster 2005) is the latest policy report to advocate that FE improve its teaching and learning by giving employers a greater role in determining its provision.

The economics of FE

A third set of stories is more specifically about the economics of FE. Some of these are concerned with ways in which FE can positively influence national economic growth. They include arguments about 'upskilling' the workforce to meet the needs of business and to ensure a healthy national economy in the context of increasing global competition, leading the economy into new growth sectors and realising the economic potential of FE in its own right as a commodified service. However, they also overlap with the previous clusters of stories, particularly around using education to avoid welfare expenditure on young people. As an example, the FEU (1991) addressed the development of 'flexible colleges' in response to the ever more fluid needs of the labour market. Interestingly, flexible colleges were devised as a *pedagogic* structure, not an *organisational* one. The shift to 'learning by doing' and competency-based assessments was to be universalised in FE, as a response to the shifting sands of the labour market.

Other stories are concerned with minimising the cost of FE itself to the national economy: the effective marketing of FE; the funding of the sector, accountability and audit; minimising resources through various forms of 'self-directed' learning; new managerialism and the deprofessionalisation/reprofessionalisation of FE teachers' work. For example, the National Audit Office conducted a study to improve value for money in FE (Bourn 2001) and as part of this, delved some way into the practices of teachers (recommending, for example, that assignments should be redesigned so as to ensure there was a lower student dropout, and therefore lower wastage of resources). The purpose of FE is defined here in terms of maximum output for minimum resources, and the pedagogy follows from this. Pursaill (1989) provides another example, commending the rapid progress of the industrial lead bodies in the late 1980s as they developed qualifications (NVQs) that would lead to the 'abolition of time-serving' by students doing courses in things they could already do well enough for the workplace. In such stories, the purpose of FE is to *cheapen* the costs of training labour while simultaneously ensuring young people's socialisation for the workplace, and pedagogy is, seemingly, expected to flow from this.

These largely indirect exhortations to improve teaching and learning therefore entail two conflicting assumptions, which we would argue continue to plague the sector. The first is that FE should provide effective responses – sometimes solutions – to a diverse array of major social, industrial and economic needs. The second is that this should be achieved with ever-increasing efficiency. Pedagogy is little more than the 'pharmakos' here (Girard 1977), the scapegoat paraded through these tales but then expelled from them.

Levers for improving teaching and learning

Little as most of these accounts have to say about *how* teaching and learning might be improved, they sometimes promote mechanisms or levers for improving teaching and learning, in which certain notions of pedagogy are implicit. These range from debates about liberal studies, competence-based learning, ICT-based learning, key skills, and the diagnosis of learning styles, to the creeping commodification of FE and proposals for its privatisation through the European General Agreement on Trade in Services (GATS).

The current GATS negotiations on education services are about which countries will offer up which parts of their education provision to the international market of providers under the terms of international free trade (Robertson 2003). While there is little awareness in the UK education community of these negotiations to privatise FE fully, they are likely to have a dramatic impact on the sector – not least due to the investment of private capital for the explicit purpose of making gains in line with the average rate of international profit across all sectors. GATS is presented as a lever that will modernise the 'delivery' of FE, but this is a policy-level discussion which is disconnected from teaching and learning practices, rendering them unproblematic. However, terms like 'delivery' belie strong and particular notions of pedagogy. One can talk of parcels being 'delivered'; increasingly, people talk of whole services being 'delivered'. It is a short step from 'the delivery of FE' to a language that many FE practitioners and educationalists find at best unrealistic or at worst dehumanising: such a language equates learning with 'delivery of the curriculum', and prescribed lists of 'learning outcomes' or competences are seen as the discrete, measurable components of learning. The effects of GATS on the pedagogy of FE are likely to be profound, but remain largely unacknowledged and unconsidered.

In the TLC project as a whole, we were more concerned with trying to understand practices 'on the ground' than with developing a detailed critique of policy (though the latter always has a bearing on the former). We were therefore just as concerned with unofficial discourses about FE, and how some elements of the debates and issues outlined above come to be felt among teaching professionals themselves. We were able to find out about this through having a relatively long association with most of the learning sites, and through the intensive participation of FE teachers – including some with long careers in the sector – in the TLC project. Our analysis suggests that in colleges, and specifically in the discussions and practices of tutors and managers, a set of three levers for improving teaching and learning in FE are prevalent. They are usually overlapping when expressed or enacted, but for the sake of clarity they are presented below as three 'ideal-types'.

'Subject' levers

Many FE teachers may be regarded, and may see themselves, as subject specialists – whether in an academic or vocational area. Improving teaching and learning starts from the assumption that the teacher's role is to induct students into the subject. Improving teaching and learning may centre on: selective recruitment of students who are better attuned to the course in some way; better resources or facilities; industry-standard equipment; greater exposure to the realities of

relevant workplaces or instances of higher-level study; more opportunities for teaching staff to engage in subject-specific updating.

'Management' levers

For others, the guiding notion is that models developed in the disciplines
of management are an effective route to improvement. For example,
a systems view sees improvement as changing the relationship of
inputs and outputs. Systematic ways of identifying needs and learning
preferences (such as Individual Learning Plans, and Learning Styles
questionnaires) can lead to processes that respond appropriately to
individual learners and therefore maximise outputs (in the form of
retention and achievement). Often incorporating the language of 'student centred', this approach to improvement has a strong affinity with
competence-based assessment, with now-established funding mechanisms and with current practices of audit and inspection against
national standards.

'Pedagogic' levers

Some people in FE, and particularly those interested in teacher education and professional development, see improvement as available
through giving attention to models of teaching and learning. There are
some important subdivisions here, in that the theoretical anchorage can
vary greatly. Psychologically derived models of learning are the most
dominant, but humanistic and also critical or emancipatory models
are also quite widespread, particularly through the influence of adult
education. What all have in common is their insistence that improving
teaching depends on the appropriate adoption and practice of particular
theories of learning. Research evidence has a role to play in helping to
consider what is or is not appropriate in the wide range of options.

   Our analysis suggests that these three ideal-types of levers (*subject,
management* and *pedagogic*) frame much of the thinking, debate and
action around the improvement of teaching and learning in colleges.
However, there are three additional themes, which we might term commonly expressed barriers to improvement, that cross-cut them. The first
is a theme of *general decline*, sometimes specifically linked to academic
standards, the amount of time available, resources, staff autonomy,
social respect for teachers, or the quality of life for students. The second
is a theme of *fragmentation and uniqueness*, so that each part of the
diverse work (or each cluster of the diverse work) of the college is seen

as entirely different and legitimately separate from all the others, so that blanket recipes for improvement have no place in FE. The third, related to the second, is in the *clustering of staff* into mutually supportive units with whom they spend much of their work time (and in some cases, leisure time) producing a strong, localised learning culture that is highly resistant to change. Our data suggests that these last two themes represent a reaction to the prevalence of the 'management' levers mentioned above.[3]

We turn now to look at some particular moments in the history of improving teaching and learning in FE, when pedagogical change (or continuity) has been both visible and significant, with a detailed analysis of two such moments.

Pedagogical change: critical moments in improving teaching and learning

Since the mid-1950s there have been a number of turning points, or critical moments, where ideas of pedagogy, and ideas about improving teaching and learning, came to the fore in FE and took a new direction. Among the most important would be the introduction of Liberal Studies in craft and technician courses, and its replacement with General Studies and Communication Studies, and subsequent redefinitions of core skills, then key skills (Hammond 2001). Another would be the introduction of competency-based qualifications which were said to promise the emergence of new and more inclusive forms of pedagogy (Jessup 1991), although they have since been criticised for reducing teaching to the assessment of competency, wherever and however that was 'learned' (see, for example, Hyland 1997; Tarrant 2000; James and Diment 2003). Within the space available here, however, we confine ourselves to examining one such key moment in detail, a turning point in which there was notably open and visible debate about pedagogy and learning, and in which some of the tensions in trying to effect such change in FE were particularly clear.

The early 1980s: A Basis for Choice

As we have already noted, the mid-1970s marked a major turning point in the history of FE itself, as the curriculum and pedagogy came under intense scrutiny and development. Traditional FE was characterised as inflexible, irrelevant, elitist, and unresponsive to the needs of young people in less advantaged situations than typical craft apprentices (Silver 1988). The didactic nature of its pedagogy was sharply criticised:

> The present position with respect to vocational courses in FE is that there still exists a widespread and strong adherence to the practice of traditional teaching approaches . . . where learning is largely teacher-directed and the learning outcomes are predominantly teacher-controlled and in which the primary role of the teacher is that of a disseminator of information.
>
> (Heathcote et al. 1982: 111)

The call for improving teaching and learning specifically in relation to the world of work was most famously expressed at this time by James Callaghan in his 'Great Debate' speech at Ruskin College in Oxford in 1976, followed by the Green Paper of 1977 (Department of Education and Science (DES) 1977). Although these were directed primarily at schooling, the same concerns were directed at FE.

The *drivers* for these changes were predominantly external. The collapse of the youth labour market in tandem with the 1973 global recession led to huge numbers of non-traditional students entering FE as a way of avoiding unemployment, rather than making positive educational or career choices. At the same time, employers were pressurising FE to respond to the post-Fordist shift in industrial organisation; and there were political imperatives to rationalise the plethora of pre-vocational courses that had sprung up.

The prime *lever* for change was the introduction of new curricula intended 'to bring about *an organised improvement in the quality of teaching and learning*' (Heathcote et al. 1982: 44, emphasis added). This focused attention, research and development centrally on pedagogy in FE. For the first time, counterposed to the dominant view of learning as didactic transmission and acquisition of cognitive knowledge and practical skills, we see a constructivist view of learning that is still about acquisition, but which is student centred, has a social aspect, and is concerned with empowering the learner.

The Further Education Curriculum Review and Development Unit (FECRDU) was set up at Coombe Lodge FE Staff College by the FEU, and in 1979, it published a document which had a major influence on this process: *A Basis for Choice* (*ABC*) (FECRDU 1979). This document (and a subsequent series developing its approach) outlined a framework for vocational preparation provision. Its stated intention was to make FE respond inclusively to its new population: the 50 per cent of 16–19 year olds with mainly negative experiences of compulsory schooling, no prospects in the labour market, and little vocational focus. In contrast to more recent policy directions (see below), *ABC* argued that FE should serve a range of purposes – moral, social, political, economic and environmental. This was framed in a powerful rhetoric of social justice and the empowerment of learners. FE should help learners develop informed career choices, it should challenge the academic–vocational divide, and it should integrate a 'core' of general education into vocational education.

ABC proposed explicit prescriptions for changes in curriculum content, pedagogical strategies and teacher roles. Content was to be defined in terms of processes rather than specified skills and knowledge, and outcomes in terms of a core of 'transferable skills', such as attitudes, values, personal qualities, 'knowing about the world of work' and basic skills. New pedagogical approaches emphasised experiential learning, discovery rather than didactic exposition, and the development of new and more 'equalised' forms of teacher–student relationships, with the assumption that these would develop desirable characteristics in students. Group activities supported by individual tutorial work, and negotiated learning outcomes, were privileged.

ABC also advocated cross-college integration of subjects that blurred subject–discipline boundaries and required teachers to work in interdisciplinary teams. It argued for greater autonomy for teachers to practise the 'art' of teaching, i.e. to relate methods to content flexibly based on diagnosis of student needs. It also recommended the recording of non-measurable achievements as a form of assessment. Such pedagogical changes were being introduced not only in the development of pre-vocational provision, but also across mainstream vocational provision in FE at the same time. While this shift appeared to challenge the ownership of FE's curriculum by industry via central examining authorities, and devolve its control to colleges and teachers to an unprecedented degree, some argued that the opposite was in fact happening: awarding bodies and industrial interests were for the first time intervening directly not just into the *content* of learning but into *learning processes and situations* themselves (Russell 1981).

This created tensions and contestation. The focus of *ABC* was on 'preparation for working life', without preparation for work per se. Crucially, this was at a time when there were very few jobs available, and little hope of employment for less advantaged young people. Yet most funding for the 'new cohort' entering FE was controlled by the Manpower Services Commission, a government agency outside the structures of FE and beyond local education authority control, which demanded that the curriculum focus on job-specific skills for labour market entry. In addition, *ABC* brought together pedagogic elements from contrasting sources. Much of it drew on critical and emancipatory perspectives which advocated recognition of students as 'people-in-the-world' and of Further Education's broader social purpose (Malcolm and Zukas 2000), to mitigate the effects of economic crisis on the most disadvantaged youth. At the same time, its focus on pedagogical innovation still assumed that diagnostic precision of individual learners' needs and teaching techniques would intrinsically foster democratic relations in the learning site and would have positive outcomes for the students.

Many people in Further Education saw this as a policy of preparing young people for a world of work which was unprepared to accept them, and noticed that this made a *social* problem look and feel like it was a problem of *individual deficits*. Colleges were trying to achieve the contradictory goals of implementing a democratic curriculum model which could empower young people, while at the same time socialising them to accept unemployment. For radical critics of *ABC* (for example, Avis 1983), the policy assumed falsely that educational interventions could solve structural social and economic problems, and that there was a correspondence between the needs of industry and those of students. Through its informal assessment regime of profiling and recording achievement, they argued that it sought to colonise students' consciousness and reform their dispositions in terms of qualities desirable to employers.

In a similar vein, Moore (1984) identified key flaws in the new vocational and pre-vocational curricula. They attributed an intrinsic ideology and values to particular types of teaching methods, and assumed naively that non-traditional, non-didactic approaches to teaching and learning are inherently radical and in the interests of working-class youth. With particular relevance to the concerns of the TLC project, such an assumption fundamentally leaves *culture* out of the equation, although – as the chapters which follow show – it is in the explicit management of the learning culture that particular learning sites are rendered more or less democratic or empowering. It does not follow that learning is more democratic or empowering just because it makes use of young people's own experiences. Arguably, in appropriating young people's experiences without exploring their material basis in, for example, class inequalities or gender-stereotyping, the kind of pedagogy promoted by *ABC* could be *dis*empowering (see Colley et al. 2003b; Colley 2006; Colley et al. 2007; see also Chapter 5 of this book).

Despite these debates, there is no doubt that the changes inspired by *ABC* focused centrally on pedagogy and new understandings of learning itself in FE. They paralleled contemporaneous changes in schooling towards more experiential forms of learning and assessment by course-work as well as terminal examinations. We would argue that critical moments like that encapsulated in *ABC* leave their mark on learning cultures at the more generic, sectoral and institutional levels, and certainly many of the tutors who participated in TLC espoused its democratic, inclusive and emancipatory aspirations. We move on, how-ever, to compare a key contemporary shift in FE policy with the focus on pedagogy epitomised by *ABC*.

Back to the future? Twenty-first-century 14–19 educational policy

In the case of 14–19 provision (which is of course only one part of what happens in FE colleges) the government chose not to follow the recommendations of the Tomlinson Report (Working Group on 14–19 Reform 2004) towards a unified system of qualifications. Nevertheless, it put in train a programme for the rapid development of new 'spe-cialised diplomas' that will require high levels of collaboration and orchestration between providers. Whether or not this is successful (or even possible) depends on a great deal more than the willingness of managers and teachers in colleges and schools to work together. The *Nuffield Review of 14–19 Education and Training* characterises the current situation as 'divided (in both curricular and institutional terms), competitive and "weakly collaborative"', arguing that '[p]olicy steering mechanisms (for example, funding, inspection, performance measures, targets, planning mechanisms and initiatives) currently support both collaboration and competition and thus ensure that current 14–19 collaborative arrangements remain weak' (Hayward et al. 2005: 172). Moreover, the same study points out that patterns of participation in FE colleges, schools and sixth form colleges 'reflect a deeply divided system':

> [F]ull-time provision for 16–19 year-old learners is largely divided along institutional and ability lines. School sixth forms and sixth form colleges are the main providers of level 3 provision, the majority of which is A level . . . FE colleges provided just under a third of level three provision, with the largest single type being NVQ and equivalent qualifications (for example, BTEC). Level 2

provision and below, on the other hand, is mainly offered by FE colleges. . . . These patterns reflect a deeply divided system based on a process of 16-plus selection. Schools and sixth form colleges cater mainly for students on higher level programmes, which suggests a process of weeding out lower level learners. Learners on Level 1 provision are taught almost exclusively in FE colleges, which have a much bigger spread of learners across the different levels than other post-16 providers.

(Hayward et al. 2005: 136)

A common-sense appreciation of this deep division might see it as separate issue from how people teach and learn. However, as we have said elsewhere in this book, it is very clear indeed in the analysis of the TLC project that the *positioning* and the *relationships between* institutions and learning sites can never be safely relegated to mere 'context'. For students and tutors in vocational courses, general education (academic) provision often provides the reference point for level, recognition and legitimacy (for example, equivalence is almost always expressed via GCSEs and A levels). The curriculum content, learning activities and assessment processes will often be defined through the ways in which they mirror or depart from those of GCSE and A level provision (for example, the proportions of examinations and assessed coursework). This issue is sometimes described as a problem of 'parity of esteem', as if it could be remedied with some targeted reform aimed at raising the status of vocational qualifications. However, its roots are cultural, linked to the way education and social class reproduce social structures. The point here is that the *positioning* of a course or qualification in relation to others becomes part of the content and process of what is actually learnt.

Earlier in this chapter, when looking at the example of the Crowther Report, we suggested that teaching and learning had a 'shadowy presence' in the diagnosis, but then become a central part of the remedy that FE could supply to a wide range of problems located either within FE itself, or in the wider economy and society. At the time of writing, this pattern is about to be played out again. In 2005 Sir Andrew Foster published a report commissioned by the Secretary of State, entitled *Realising the Potential: A review of the future role of further education colleges* (Foster 2005). The review was wide-ranging, although – just like Crowther – it did not include an explicit focus on understanding and improving teaching and learning. Its remit was closely tied to the reform agenda already in train around 14–19 and the Skills Strategy. Foster was

> to consider issues raised by the reform agenda for colleges of
> Further Education . . . [including] Ethos, mission and structure;
> Workforce, leadership and governance; Relationships with other
> providers, schools and universities; Employer engagement;
> Business planning and income generation; Systems to disseminate
> best practice and enhance the reputation of the sector.
>
> (Foster 2005: 108)

The Foster review made many detailed recommendations pertaining to
all these terms of reference. One of its overall conclusions was that
'[a]bove all, FE lacks a clearly recognised and shared core purpose' and
that 'the way forward in resolving these causes [*sic*] includes an appetite
to catch up with competitive international economies' and 'a conse-
quential core focus on skills and employability' (Foster 2005: 6). Soon
after, drawing on the review and upon several other policy developments, a White Paper (*Further Education: Raising skills, improving life
chances*: DfES 2006) sets out a 'new' vision by way of response:

> The FE system must be the powerhouse for delivering the skills at
> all levels that are needed to sustain an advanced, competitive
> economy and make us a fairer society, offering equal opportunities
> for all based on talent and effort, not background.
>
> (DfES 2006: Executive Summary para. 3)

This can be recognised as combining both the 'social cohesion' and 'economics' stories outlined earlier in this chapter. The White Paper contains
a whole section on 'a national strategy for teaching and learning in
Further Education'. This sets out a new emphasis on self-improvement
for 'driving up quality' and for delivering a 'more personalised service'
for learners. The new Quality Improvement Agency will provide a more
coherent support than has been available hitherto, when its concerns
were spread across some five different agencies. Teaching staff will be
supported with new materials and subject coaches, and, in addition
to the requirements introduced in 2004 for a teaching qualification,
new measures will support the development of the workforce, with a
continuing professional development requirement. Other new initiatives
will do more to attract graduates and experienced managers to the
sector, to develop leadership skills and to address diversity issues in
the workforce.

Thus, while teaching and learning is the topic of a whole chapter, the
White Paper is primarily concerned with the agencies, frameworks and

mechanisms which it is hoped will 'drive up quality', rather than saying anything – beyond the odd reference to learning styles and personalisation – about the nature of effective teaching and learning. *ABC* may have represented a step forward, but FE policy has taken two steps back. Despite first impressions, the 'silence' identified by Coffield (see p. 44) has not been broken.

Conclusion

In a sense, then, FE colleges can be thought of as historical tapestries that, in addition to being made of local or regional fabric, tell us which parts of greater stories – about curriculum, qualifications, improvement – have been in town, which ones have disappeared, and which have stayed on. Some parts of the image have been reworked many times. Other parts have been unpicked, forcibly erased, and we have needed to do some 'archaeology' in order to reconstruct the whole picture. This is the background against which the TLC tutors attempted to transform the learning cultures – and thereby improve teaching and learning – in their own sites, as we explain in Chapter 6. It is also the terrain in which particular learning cultures are generated and enacted, as we shall begin to explore in Chapter 4.

Notes

1   'Whisky money' refers to a period in which the taxation raised against whisky sales was used to fund FE.
2   'Incorporation' refers to the removal of FE colleges from local authority control and their reconstitution as marketised businesses funded directly by centralised agencies and mechanisms.
3   We are particularly grateful to Michael Tedder for the input he provided on the analysis of professional experiences for this section.

Chapter 4

Learning cultures across sites

Introduction

There are very many different types of learning culture in FE – far too many to describe them all in this chapter.[1] The root cause of this diversity is that every single feature that influences a learning culture varies in its form and impact from site to site. It follows that it is possible to classify types of learning culture according to many of these factors. Thus, we could classify cultures according to the types of students in them – older or younger, part-time or full-time, predominantly female, predominantly male, or mixed gender, different levels of prior educational attainment, different social class backgrounds, etc. Alternatively we could classify sites according to curriculum content: academic or vocational, different types of vocational, different levels of target qualification, etc. There may well be good reasons for doing any of these, and many other possible classificatory factors could be listed. This, however, is an unhelpful approach from a cultural point of view because whereas all such potential variables can be important to a greater or lesser extent in all cultures, none is universally pre-eminent. More seriously, taking one such prime variable risks marginalising the significance of others and underestimating the relational nature of the learning.

In this chapter we have taken three rather different approaches. First, we look at our sites on the basis of the quantitative data we collected through our survey sweeps. Second, based upon all our data, we examine different types of relationships between factors as a way of grouping sites. Third, we examine exemplar clusters of sites where several factors coalesce in similar ways. In each case, it is important to remember that even when cultures are very similar, the specific unique features of

Authored by Phil Hodkinson, Gert Biesta, Keith Postlethwaite and Wendy Maull

the culture of each learning site remain and can be of fundamental importance.

Positioning learning sites and characterising learning cultures

As well as providing the data to enable us to map the demographic characteristics of the students (see Chapter 1), our questionnaire also contained a number of questions selected from the *Constructivist Learning Environment Survey* (CLES) (Taylor et al. 1997). The selected questions were those which comprised three of the original subscales of CLES, namely Critical Voice, Shared Control and Student Negotiation. The questions we included were therefore:

Critical Voice

- It's OK for me to complain about activities that are confusing.
- It's OK for me to ask the tutor 'Why do I have to learn this?'
- It's OK for me to express my opinion.
- It's OK for me to question the way I'm being taught.

Shared Control

- I help the tutor to plan what I am going to do.
- I help the tutor to decide what activities are best for me.
- I help the tutor to plan which activities I do.
- I help the tutor to assess my learning.

Student Negotiation

- I get the chance to talk to other students.
- Other students explain their ideas to me.
- I explain my ideas to other students.
- I ask other students to explain their ideas.
- Other students ask me to explain my ideas.
- I talk with other students about how to solve problems.

Although, for Cohort 1, there were no significant differences among sites in terms of Critical Voice, analysis of variance indicated several groupings of sites in terms of Student Negotiation and Shared Control. These are summarised in Figure 4.1. The solid horizontal and vertical lines represent divisions between groups of sites based on the

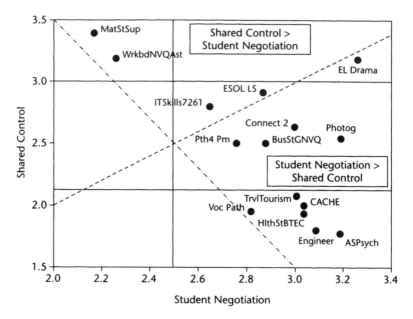

Figure 4.1 Mean scores for Shared Control and Student Negotiation for each learning site

statistically significant differences in means revealed by Tukey HSD post-hoc tests that were used as part of the analysis of variance.

The Entry Level Drama (EL Drama) site was the only site to have especially high Shared Control and high Student Negotiation scores. However, there is some doubt about the extent to which this particular group of students understood the CLES questions,[2] so this site is not included in the following discussion (for more information on this site, see the textbox later on in this chapter).

The downward sloping chain-dotted line in Figure 4.1 shows an apparent threshold for Shared Control + Student Negotiation below which the sites did not fall. The existence of this threshold indicates that there was no site in which students perceived an environment of both low Shared Control and low Student Negotiation. It appears that, in all our sites, students on average felt able to exchange ideas with somebody, either the tutor or other students. Whereas this is not surprising if we regard a learning site as having an important social dimension, it does provide evidence that students' responses to the questionnaire reflected this social aspect of their learning environment.

The upward sloping line in Figure 4.1 separates sites where Shared Control was greater than Student Negotiation, from those for which it was less. As is clear from the fact that most sites lie below this line, Student Negotiation scores were almost always higher than Shared Control scores, indicating that, in most sites, students found it easier to share their ideas with their peers than to influence the way they were taught through discussion with their tutor. However, in the IT Skills 7261, Mature Students Support (MatStSup), Work-based NVQ Assessment (WrkbdNVQAst) and ESOL Learning Services (ESOL LS) sites, the Shared Control scores were higher than the Student Negotiation scores. Looking at the qualitative data from individual sites we could account for this in terms of pedagogical practice or site organisation influencing the perceived learning environment. In the Mature Students Support site, for example, high Shared Control may have been related to the fact that the one-to-one support provided involved initial assessment of a student through a self-assessment questionnaire on technical skills, or negotiation with the student based on evidence from assignments, and the construction of 'learning plans' that were agreed and reviewed by the tutor and student, and signed after each tutorial. In other sites low Student Negotiation may have been a consequence of the students' geographical isolation from one another in different workplaces (Work-based NVQ Assessment), or a reflection of difficulties in inter-student communication arising from students' insecurity in the use of English and the different first languages that they spoke (ESOL Learning Services). In the IT Skills 7261 site the tutor expected students to organise their own work and plan the time to be devoted to different aspects within an overall framework created by the awarding body; students visited the site when they needed to, so they did not meet other students as a consistent group. Given the nature of the questions on these scales, these characteristics would be expected to lead to high Shared Control and low Student Negotiation respectively, which is, roughly, where this site is indeed positioned (see Figure 4.1).

It is tempting to stop the discussion for a given site once a quantitative effect has been 'explained' in this way by a relevant qualitative description for that site. However, what is particularly intriguing is that, in *any* of these sites, and especially for one or more individuals in these sites, the processes leading to the learning culture being perceived as one where Shared Control was higher than Student Negotiation may have been a complex interweaving of any or all of the factors identified *across this subgroup of sites as a whole*. Some students in *any* of these sites may have discussed an individual work plan with the tutor; some students in *any* of these sites may have felt that there were few opportunities to discuss work with their peers. By grouping the sites together, the quantitative strand therefore encouraged us to look across the qualitative data for each subset of sites, to tease out the widest range of factors that might help us to understand the learning cultures of those sites in all their complexity.

The grouping of sites also helped us to deepen our understanding of what an individual factor might mean. Consider the factor of isolation. This factor came immediately to mind in understanding low Student Negotiation in the Work-based NVQ Assessment 'site', which consisted of a tutor visiting different workplaces to assess students, because in that site students were isolated by geography. The physical isolation in the Work-based NVQ Assessment site was not reproduced elsewhere, but we were drawn by the grouping of the sites to recognise that the language issue in the ESOL site could also be seen as leading to isolation, in this case linguistic isolation. Further, we felt that there might be isolation by programme structure in the IT Skills 7261 and Mature Student Support sites where students joined and left the course as they needed to (so that although students shared a geographical base, there may or may not have been other students in that base at any particular time).

If isolation, seen in these broad terms, helped to explain the perceived learning culture of this set of sites, it was then interesting to ask whether other sites identified quantitatively as significantly different from this group, were seen, by the researchers who knew the sites well, to encompass any aspect of isolation. Researchers in the six sites in the lower right hand corner of Figure 4.1 (that is, those which formed the most strongly contrasting group) were asked to reflect on this: in four sites they responded indeed that isolation was 'not at all evident in this site'. This analysis led us to the view that isolation may be an important influence on perceived learning culture, reducing the perception that negotiation with peers was a significant part of learning.

The issues discussed above were further explored by studying similar data for the second cohort of students in the learning sites (see also Postlethwaite and Maull 2003). Although the position of sites did change in the diagram, most remained in the 'box' in which they were placed on the basis of Cohort 1 data. However, two sites – IT Skills 7261 and Vocational Pathways – were exceptions. At the start of Cohort 2, these two sites had moved into the bottom left hand corner of Figure 4.1, having low Shared Control *and* Low Student Negotiation scores. They therefore challenged our view, based on Cohort 1 data, that discussion of some sort (with tutor or with peers) was always a characteristic of our sites. Interestingly, the qualitative researchers responsible for these sites argued that in both of them Cohort 2 started their year much less effectively than Cohort 1, suggesting that a lack of perceived opportunities for discussion in Cohort 2 was associated with a less effective learning culture.

As well as studying differences between successive cohorts of students, we also monitored change over time (one or two years) within cohorts. One interesting finding was that Student Negotiation scores fell quite sharply in a site where two cliques emerged within the student body – perhaps emphasising yet another aspect of isolation: namely isolation by choice – the establishment of subgroups which then reduced opportunities for sharing among the students. This proved the point that learning cultures not only are constructed by pedagogy and curriculum, but also depend on the actions of the participants, in this case the students in a particular culture. More generally, there were many statistically significant differences in perceived learning environment scores during students' lifetimes in their learning sites. As we have explained elsewhere (Postlethwaite and Maull 2007), in each site the qualitative data enabled us to identify factors which might explain each of these changes. However, as argued above, it was not the main purpose of the survey to suggest that a given factor had a given effect in a given site, but rather to identify the range of possible influences on the perceived learning culture in sites generally. Clearly tutors *can* make a difference to the learning culture of a site, but other factors outside their control also make a difference. Broader issues such as management style, changing staff responsibilities, teaching team stability, the development of alternative provision by other providers, student grouping policy, course choice, admissions policy, resource changes or site location all had an effect. Our focus on particular combinations of scores on Shared Control and Student Negotiation scores helped us to build up an understanding of significant and relevant differences between learning cultures. Interrogation of the qualitative data then helped to identify factors related to these differences. This is not to say that these were the only factors that make a difference. In the next two sections we therefore look at other dimensions that helped us to understand similarities and differences between learning cultures.

Cultures of convergence and synergy

Brown et al. (1989) wrote a seminal article setting out the differences between what they termed authentic or everyday learning and learning in school. Authentic learning occurred when, in their terms, concepts, contexts and activities were mutually supportive – in synergy. School learning, they argued, was less effective, because the concepts being taught were at odds with the context (a school) and with the activities (student tasks, rather than everyday practice). This point about synergy should not be misunderstood. Brown et al. (1989) do not claim that everyday life is without conflict. Indeed, it could be argued that employment within a capitalist system has conflicts between the interests of capital and labour at its heart. Similarly, when we talk of synergistic learning cultures within the TLC data, we should not be interpreted as implying that similar underlying conflicts are somehow absent. What we do mean is that *many* of the factors that influence learning are convergent – they are pulling in similar directions that complement and reinforce each other. Where this convergence is strong, the result can be synergistic.

If we examine some of those TLC learning cultures where convergence and synergy are strongest, there is some initial support for this focus on synergy, but not for the assumption that learning in educational institutions always lacks it. In the CACHE site (Child Care and Education), for example, much of the learning culture was convergent and synergistic, and geared towards learning to become a nursery nurse. Similarly, in the Entry Level Drama course (see pp. 67–68), there was a strong convergence of dispositions, attitudes and pressures, towards what can be described as not only learning and enjoying being in a play, but also learning and enjoying being in a second family. In the online basic IT skills site there was a strong convergence also. This time, there was a complex blend of simple structured curriculum and learning tasks, complex and technical systems of record-keeping, assignment logging, etc., tutors who were at the end of a phone or email constantly within office hours, a tutorial approach that used primarily the phone and emails to develop caring relationships with individual students, and students themselves who were (very) part-time, did not want to come in to college, and did not want this course to impinge too much on their lives or identity.

The Entry Level Drama site

The Entry Level Drama site catered for students aged between 16 and 23, regarded as having moderate to severe learning disabilities, studying drama on a one-year full-time course. The site was characterised by a synergy between two forms of practice and identity. The first was preparing for and performing in a dramatic production. The tutor determined the nature of the play and the day-to-day tasks and activities. Other externally determined objectives, such as learning basic numeracy and literacy skills, were tied in to this overall dramatic production. Performance was a key purpose of the course. The course had two explicit educational goals: to learn drama and to learn skills that would increase employability. This entailed a fixed one-year time frame, externally set objectives, and assessment and qualification through a portfolio-based scheme. Participation entailed the experience-based holistic engagement of the students in the play itself and in a series of practical exercises and activities. Students were pleased to be actors, and to be part of a production. They learned how to do drama. This became a (temporary) part of their identities.

The second form of practice and identity was that of a 'second family'. The students actively constructed this by treating tutors as surrogate parents, who were pressured to sort out any difficulties, problems or arguments. The tutors took on a much more protective, caring pastoral role for these students than for others, including, for example, supervising them at lunchtime, when the students went to the canteen, but did not mix outside their own group. The students' growing self-confidence and ability in areas such as interpersonal communication were bounded by this family context. They learned how to behave in this setting, with these particular fellow students (siblings) and these particular tutors (parents).

The 'family' and the 'theatre company' aspects were completely integrated. Both were structured by and themselves structure the relative isolation of the group, in one mobile classroom. Students were there all the time, some tutors came and went, but the teaching team was small. This was home and rehearsal room. This combination co-constructed a hidden curriculum of increasing dependency and safety, with minimal risk or challenge. The family identity constrained and tamed the theatre company, and the tutors made more

continued

allowances for these students than for those on other drama courses. Formal assessment was relatively painless, with no externally set high-performance thresholds to increase anxiety and the risk of failure. The final production was only for parents and close friends, and in one year not even parents were invited, as the tutor felt that to have an audience would be too demanding for some students (the family) and risk an unpolished performance (the theatre company). Despite the rhetoric of learning for employability and progression, the students mainly went on to participate in similar entry level courses. This is because there was no easily accessible labour market for students like these. Thus, an implicit and hidden purpose of the course could be described as warehousing with productive and self-fulfilling engagement.

Very many of the factors that influence learning were convergent in this site, resulting in a broadly synergistic learning culture. Students were happy. Tutors were happy. Inspectors were happy. As far as we can tell, parents were happy. The college was not really interested, but was broadly happy, because inspection results were excellent, the course brought in high levels of funding, and had high rates of retention and achievement. The government was happy, because the students were productively occupied, and its official targets were being met.

In these and other sites with broadly 'synergistic' learning cultures, we could identify successful learning. These are some of the sites where learning was most effective. Indeed, as will be more fully explored later, one very important way to improve learning effectiveness is to look for ways to increase synergy in the learning culture. But in each case, there was a price, if the second question about the value of what is being learned is also asked. In the CACHE course, linked in as it was to the vocational culture of the child care profession, issues of female gender stereotyping, emotional labour, low status and poor pay were enshrined and unchallenged, and learned by the students (Colley et al. 2003b). Only in the area of equality of opportunity related to ethnicity, did a combination of tutor commitment and government legislation facilitate any sort of critical challenge to the status quo. In entry level drama, the price was the further isolation of the students from the rest of the college and the local community, and the reinforcement of their dependency and infantilisation. The students themselves worked for this, while also wishing that they were more like other people. In the online basic IT skills course, there was limited student investment and little therefore to lose. However, the costs to the tutors was high, for the nature of the provision cut them off from all other types of teaching, from teacher training, and from the chance to enhance their status from technician to qualified teacher. This was because they had to be present in the same office, in front of the same computer, for the full working day.

Furthermore, in most synergistic sites, that very synergy was constructed at a cost to some students, through subtle processes of exclusion, to remove some sources of divergence or possible tension. In CACHE, this happened in a variety of ways. Some students were forced to leave, because they were deemed to be unsuitable for the profession (for example, because of a police caution). Others were encouraged to leave, as not really fitting in. Also, during the fieldwork, the entry requirements were raised, primarily in response to issues of status equivalence. The result was to improve the work ethic of the group, reduce some of the pressures on the tutors (fewer struggling students to support) and produce better final assessment results. The entry level drama group did not exclude in that way at all. However, as we have seen, its success was built upon separating out certain types of student from the rest of the student body. (Interestingly, the site was arguably at its strongest in the third year of data collection, when a relatively more diverse group of students was recruited.) The online basic IT skills provision was the exception here. The student population was incredibly diverse, sharing only a commitment to learning to use a computer.

Such synergy is sometimes a fragile construction. In AS French, for example, there was a strong synergy of dispositions between tutor and students, the FE location, the pedagogical approaches adopted, and the performance nature of speaking a foreign language. In the first year of our research, the main divergent tendencies came from the pressure to get through a difficult academic syllabus in just over two terms, and a wide variation in prior French ability in the students, which caused the tutor to partially move away from teaching entirely in the target language. However, in the second year, a combination of circumstances resulted in a halving of the student contact time, and in the tutor deciding to take voluntary redundancy. This suggests that the initial synergy was achieved at considerable cost to the tutor and that the later halving of contact time was a final straw that increased this cost to a level that was unbearable to that tutor. CACHE faced potential problems in the future, too. This was a two-year course, which had been allowed by the college to measure its retention rates from early in the students' second year. Starting just after the research finished, retention was to be measured from early in Year 1. This could have a potentially major impact, as many students drop out or are encouraged to leave during the first year, while those who make it through into Year 2 are likely to stay until the end. Put differently, an element of divergence and possible conflict, between on the one hand, the needs of the profession for unsuitable students to be weeded out, and from an access perspective, students with weak prior academic achievements to be admitted and given a chance to succeed, clashes with performance indicator driven needs for the college to maximise student retention for the whole course.

Cultures of division and conflict

The argument about divergence and challenge promoting learning also has a long pedigree. The argument is that learning entails change, and that people are more likely to learn, to change, when faced by a new situation, problem or difficulty (see, for example, Biesta 2001, 2006). This can be illustrated in many workplaces, where the continual repetition of the same routine job provides little opportunity for learning. Thus, in different but related ways, Engeström (2001) and Fuller and Unwin (2003) argue that the best learning environments at work are expansive ones. For Engeström, this happens when two 'activity systems' overlap, this causing participants to rethink and relearn their roles. For Fuller and Unwin (2003), engaging in a range of different learning activities and situations enhances workplace learning as, for example, when an apprentice works in several different parts of a steel firm, over the two year apprenticeship.

In some of our sites, conflicts and tensions seem to be more problematic, and not of the type of constructive challenge that the workplace learning writers describe. We have space for two examples. In GNVQ Business Studies, there were strong divergences (Wahlberg and Gleeson 2003). The tutors did not really value the curriculum or the course, and would have preferred to teach something else to these students. They saw the students as not especially able and not very hard working. The students, on the other hand, though coming from diverse backgrounds, generally shared the view that this was a high-status course and that they had done well to gain admission to it. They also hoped and expected that it would lead directly to a good job. This, in turn conflicted with the structural positioning and content of the course. Though labelled 'vocational', the course had no employer or employment links.

There was no work experience, and no immediate vocational influence. Instead, the course focused on the constantly changing GNVQ syllabus and assessment, and the tutors doubted the possibility of progressing from this course to a 'good job'. Significant effort was devoted to pushing the students into behaving as if they were at work. This caused ongoing frictions, for example about (not) wearing baseball caps. All this reinforced the sense that the students were college students, not workers. This tension between being a student and being a worker could be seen in the contrasting demands of informalised, student-centred learning; a more technicist approach to learning, achieved through rigid adherence to an assessment grid; and the need to instil formal working practices, to simulate real employment. There was effective learning in this site, and many students achieved the final qualification. However, it is hard to see how the sorts of divergence and conflicts inherent in this site contributed to effective learning, rather than being barriers to it.

A second site that is epitomised by significant divergence was AS Psychology, which is more fully described in the textbox. As in GNVQ Business Studies, there was much successful learning in this site. Many of the more able students thrived and grew, in the face of the intellectual challenge. However, many of the weaker students could not cope with the pace of work nor with the level of abstract and uncertain knowledge it entailed. The tensions within this learning culture were significant, and impeded the learning of many of the students.

The AS level Psychology site

This learning site provided a part-time evening course leading to a high-level and difficult academic examination in psychology, in one year. Students enrolled in September, and the examinations took place in the following June. Psychology was a popular subject, and Jedi, the tutor, began the year with twenty-nine students, from diverse backgrounds, studying the course for different reasons, and with differing levels of prior academic attainment. The group met with Jedi for one three-hour session per week, and a considerable amount of curriculum content had to be covered very quickly. Jedi was a charismatic tutor, with a distinctive approach to the discipline. He viewed psychology as a humanities subject rather than its more typical presentation as a science, and emphasised the uncertainty of

continued

knowledge and the importance of critical evaluation in this subject, that could lead to a range of justifiable conclusions rather than to one 'correct answer'. He saw his role as giving the students a deep understanding of the nature of psychology, which could then be applied in many different contexts. This entailed giving the students a conceptual map of the discipline, and then applying that map to a series of different case study topics that were specified in the syllabus. We judged Jedi to be a very effective teacher, but of a particular type. He also got excellent ratings from an external inspection. He dominated classroom activities, but excelled at helping students participate in discussions and devoted lots of time to re-explaining things if one or more students made it clear that they did not understand. All the students found him impressive, and many learned very effectively from this approach. He had an impressive track record of success in students progressing to a second year to take a full A level course, and eventually progressing to university.

Conflicts in the learning culture arose from in-built divergences of some factors. The large and diverse student intake was reinforced by FE funding, by recruitment and retention, and by the mission in the sector to open up learning to the socially excluded. Jedi liked this diversity, and liked giving everyone a chance to succeed. However, his teaching approach was arguably better suited to working with a smaller group, where every student could be more fully engaged every week. There were also divergences around the student dispositions and the curriculum and assessment requirements. These were part-time students, who could attend for only one evening a week, and many found the academic standards required difficult to reach. Yet the curriculum content had been designed for full-time 16+ students, who would normally get far more than three hours' contact time. Historically the AS level provision was the first year of a two-year A level programme, with no formal examination at the end of year one. As a course in its own right the AS level required the achievement of high levels of academic understanding in an unprecedented short timescale. The group size further intensified these divergences, as getting through the content, while helping as many students as possible, took up a great deal of time, and added to the difficulties of finishing the course.

These in-built divergences resulted in serious conflicts for some students on the course. Though there was a very effective synergy for the most able, and for some others who attached themselves to the most able subgroup, many other students found the struggle was beyond their ability to cope, and their learning of psychology was seriously impaired. These negative effects were intensified if a student missed a session, as the pace on the course was very rapid, and the learning was essentially experiential. It was not just a matter of picking up some missing content. It was also made worse if a struggling student tried to work closely with other struggling students. Peer support then reinforced a sense of failure and difficulty, and at times resembled the blind leading the blind.

In sites like these, where tensions, divergences and even conflicts were pre-eminent in the learning culture, the main impact on learning seemed to be negative. In such cases, the tensions were dysfunctional for the site as a whole, though not necessarily so for all learners, all tutors or all learning. When we examine these sorts of analysis, the ways in which learning could be improved often entail reducing or removing conflicts – increasing convergence over divergence. The problem is that enhancing convergence is often very difficult to achieve, and almost always requires major changes that lie outside the direct control of the tutor. The GNVQ tutors could do little about the lack of fit between the course and employment practices and opportunities. The AS Psychology tutor could do nothing about the rigorous course content and assessment, or the one session per week contact time. He could, perhaps, have instituted a much more rigorous and restrictive entry requirement. However, this would have resulted in fewer students, and risked making the course uneconomic, in the college management terms. In addition, such a change would have meant a significant switch in his own professional identity – his deep belief that everyone had the right to try psychology. There are parallels here in the GNVQ site. Valuing the course and the students entailed a significant shift in the professional identity of tutors who had previously seen themselves primarily as experts in accountancy or economics. Even if such identity changes are judged to be desirable, their achievement is far from certain. As Bourdieu (Bourdieu and Wacquant 1992) shows, and as we have highlighted in Chapter 2, dispositions are deeply lodged, and difficult to change.

None of this is to claim that there is no place for challenge and divergence in FE learning, or to imply that maximising convergence is a panacea for improvement.

Mixing convergence and divergence

Instead of seeing convergence and divergence as polar ideal-types, it fits our data better to think of a rough continuum. There were significant elements of convergence and divergence in the learning cultures of all sites. In some of our sites, convergent and divergent elements of the learning culture were more equally distributed. One such site was electrical engineering. One issue is the relationship between college learning and employment practice. Both tutors and students felt that the links were poor or inadequate, but their reasons differed. Students felt that college equipment was out of date, and that what they were taught was of little direct use. The real learning was on the job – attending this day-release programme was simply a necessary chore. Most tutors, on the other hand, saw a dumbing down of proper engineering skills. They frequently talked of the terminal decline of the profession. In this, they held employers and curriculum designers equally to blame. The result was a very unhealthy synergy of cynicism towards the learning in the site. Another source of convergence and divergence lay in the nature of those involved. This was an almost entirely male and masculine site, but there was a sharp division between the youth of the students and the older age of most of the tutors, who were nearing retirement. One younger tutor was increasingly unhappy working in this site, feeling there was no way to change or improve deeply entrenched practices. Finally, there was a clear divergence between what tutors wanted out of the site – proper engineers – and what the students and their employers wanted, which was the qualification, but with minimum effort (the students) and minimum interference with working practices (the employers). The result was that the course and qualification took on the nature of a workplace rite of passage: something that young men had to endure, in order to become fully paid up members of the workforce. This compromise kept both employers and college satisfied. The former got qualified workers. The latter got satisfactory retention and achievement rates. The result was neither a healthy synergy of factors that reinforced learning, nor a deep divergence or conflict that impeded it.

Groups of similar learning cultures

It is sometimes useful to examine groups of learning cultures that are similar in some respects. There are many ways in which this can be done, depending on the purpose of the analysis. In this chapter we have chosen to illustrate the value of this type of approach by examining two groupings, made according to the well-established distinction between academic and vocational courses. We examine the learning cultures of vocational courses first.

Similarities and contrasts in vocational learning cultures

Though they are often thought of as a single group, our research identified several different types of vocational provision within FE. One key variation, which has significant implications for the learning cultures of vocational sites, is the nature of the relationship with employment. All vocational programmes require relationships with relevant employment sectors – such a relationship is implicit within the name itself. There should be a close relationship between the knowledge, skills and understanding needed in the sector and the curriculum content of a vocational education and training (VET) course or programme. In addition, VET courses either provide progression from the course into related employment or provide relevant off the job education for trainees already working in a firm. These two functions are linked, but making them work is fraught with difficulty. One indication of this complexity is that many students' original job-related expectations were not realised in four of the VET programmes studied. In another, students claimed that their job prospects had improved but not because of increased understanding of the workplace. One way of understanding some of those difficulties is to consider four different types of employment relationship which are common in FE. They are:

- College-based provision, but with integral links with local employers.
- College-based provision, but with no significant employer links.
- Employer-based modern apprenticeship provision, with some college day release.
- Employer-based provision, with college-organised assessment of NVQ competences.

Within each of these four types of employment relationship, the degree of synergy and/or conflict between the cultural practices and values of the workplace (the 'vocational culture': see Colley 2006) and the cultural practices and values within the college provision can vary. A third significant influence on the learning cultures of vocational courses derives from their multiple purposes within the UK context. National policy sees vocational provision as fulfilling four different purposes. They are:

- to develop the workforce skills needed by employers
- to provide progression into particular occupational areas
- to provide a second chance for young people who have not succeeded in academic courses
- to form an alternative form of general education, focused on employability, for full-time students between the ages of 14 and 19.

There are conflicts and tensions, as well as potential synergies between these different purposes, which are paralleled by the diversity in the reasons students have for studying these courses, and the things that they want to get out of them. Among many other variations, the following types of student disposition were common within the TLC sample:

- those who had made a specific vocational career choice
- those who had entered the course without any clear or thought-through career objective
- those who became increasingly focused on the occupational objective of the course
- those who became separated from the occupational objective of the course
- those who saw or came to see the course as a means to Further Educational study
- those who saw the course as a necessary burden to be endured and completed
- those who left partway through, for a variety of complex reasons
- those who lacked confidence and saw the vocational course as a means of re-engaging with education – a second chance.

Some students fitted into several of these types, either at the same time, or at different stages in their learning careers. All these and other student variations can be found in all four types of vocational provision, though some types of provision are more likely to attract some types of student disposition. Put differently, each of these ways of organising types of vocational learning are interrelated, exactly as the learning cultures approach would suggest.

The most effective VET provision is likely to be found when college and employer links are very close, even synergistic. We have already explored this in relation to the CACHE site within the TLC. Fuller and Unwin (2003) showed how such close links can also work very well in a modern apprenticeship scheme in the steel industry. Such vocational learning is very effective, but at a price. As we have already seen in the case of CACHE, such close synergy between employer and college values and practices makes it very difficult for college tutors to challenge or problematise the vocational culture. Furthermore, because of the tight focus on a particular occupation in the learning culture of such courses, they are less suitable for students who do not want to enter that occupation. In the CACHE example, the tightly knit focus on the practice of being a nursery nurse progressively marginalised students like this. A few dropped out and some were excluded, while others were thought by tutors to disrupt the emotional bonding of the group.

Where links between college and employers are less close, there can be different problems. With the engineering day-release course, for example, many students struggled to see the value and relevance of what was taught in the college. Their identity was formed at work, and they did not regard themselves as 'college students'. This sort of situation may allow college tutors to introduce theory and methods not found at work, and thus challenge aspects of existing working practices. However, the risk is that the more they do this, the less notice of them some students will take. Here too, emotions played a role in inclusion and exclusion, as students completed or dropped out according to their ability to endure the demands of college work in addition to full-time employment and family responsibilities.

An increasing number of VET courses have no substantial employer links or even work experience. This was the case on a GNVQ business education course (see Wahlberg and Gleeson 2003) and is likely to be the case in many successors to GNVQ. Students enrolled on a full-time course intending to learn skills to get them good jobs in business and hoping to progress into employment. Business-related knowledge, skills and understanding were successfully taught, and tutors were unconstrained by specific employment practices. However, it proved very difficult to inculcate into the students ways of behaving and working appropriate for employment. Many students had no practical experience of work in the business sector with which to relate what they were taught. The successful ones learned how to be good students of business studies, not how to be business employees. The lack of local employer links also made progression into related employment difficult for many.

Sometimes all the college does is provide NVQ assessment/verification (James and Diment 2003). What is learned depends almost entirely on the employers, and there are often problems because the normal working practices are too narrow and/or too specialised to allow the whole range of NVQ competence to be developed. In the TLC example, one college tutor took it upon herself to work with the candidates and their employers to fill as many of these gaps as possible. The result was relatively high pass rates. These were achieved because the tutor provided her candidates with a range of other activities to support their learning. This was not officially part of her job, and the college was not funded to provide it, but it was an essential ingredient in the success of the programme. College policy decisions to move to online forms of assessment (reflecting a broad national trend) closed down the space for such 'underground' tutor–student contact and the learning opportunities it could generate.

In addition to these differences between the learning cultures of different vocational sites and courses, there are also some shared features. One is the significance of status hierarchies. Fundamental to this is the long-established status difference between vocational and academic courses. This is reinforced by the ways in which vocational courses of all types are used as a second chance for students who have not done so well with mainstream academic school provision. Many students value this 'second chance' to succeed, together with the more practical and instrumental focus of the work. However, this purpose for VET serves to reinforce its inferior status. Our research also revealed complex hierarchies of status between different VET qualifications. These hierarchies are seen in the attitudes of tutors and some students, in the required entry qualifications, and in the ways that possible progression routes are described. Consequently, one of the main effects of the current VET system and its division from the academic curriculum is to reproduce and reinforce educational and employment inequalities.

Another key feature of vocational provision of all types is the tendency to reinforce rather than challenge gender stereotyping in employment and careers. That is, student recruitment onto vocational courses tends to mirror gender-based divisions of labour in the employment world. The result is that many vocational courses are either predominantly female, like nursery nurse training, or predominantly male, like engineering. Those that are mixed, such as business studies, reflect an occupation that already provides wide employment opportunities for both genders. This is one of the major ways in which the dominance of vocational cultures in the world of employment results in a conservative and socialising tendency in vocational provision.

Academic courses and learning cultures

Within the TLC, we studied two academic learning sites. One, concerning AS Psychology, has already been described; the other was AS French, which is described in the textbox.

The AS French site

AS levels are traditional academic courses at advanced level, assessed by terminal examinations, and usually taken (prior to A2 levels) in preparation for entry to Higher Education. Modern foreign languages (MFL) are regarded, along with physics and mathematics, as the most difficult AS subjects. AS French requires a good command of the written and spoken language, as well as a detailed knowledge of culture and history in the French-speaking world and a study of French literature. The students we interviewed claimed to enjoy the high status and intellectual challenge of the course.

They relished aspects of speaking French as a kind of 'performance'. On the one hand it involved risk, since mistakes in speaking French in front of a group of peers could be potentially humiliating. On the other hand, success brought with it a thrill, and the ability to communicate in a foreign language made them feel special and distinct from those many British people who cannot. This in turn is connected with a desire to experience the exotic 'elsewhere' promised by mastery of a foreign language and understanding of a foreign culture. As one student enthused, 'It's like the study of France – in French! . . . It's more than just being able to speak French, really, isn't it? Like, it's a bit of knowledge in there as well'.

These emotions were a strong feature of participating in the course, since the tutor, Florence, had an ideological commitment to conducting lessons predominantly in French. Her preference was to eschew didactic, teacher-controlled approaches, and to negotiate

---

continued

students' democratic involvement in self- and peer-conducted diagnosis and assessment. Using the target language as much as possible
served her more fundamental aims of creating an inclusive and
motivating experience for all her students – many of them had not
had the opportunity to visit France and be immersed in the language
there that more advantaged young people often have. But this
approach was also dependent on her intuitive understanding of
students' degree of comprehension, her sensitive responses to their
difficulties, and her ability to nurture a supportive culture within
the group. These aspects of her pedagogy allowed students to take
the risk of performing as French speakers in a relatively safe environment. This points to the basic synergy in this site: content, context
and activities may not cohere with the actual experience of *living* in
France, but they did cohere with the task of studying AS level French
in a college classroom.

Students' intentions could conflict with the official purposes of
the course. For many, the decision to study academic courses in FE
– rather than in a school or sixth form college – reflected their
rebellion against the stricter disciplinary regime of school. In contrast
with their tutor's aim of encouraging them to achieve their full
potential in the subject, and government targets that focus on high
levels of attendance, retention and attainment, some students
wanted to minimise the importance of education in their wider lives.
Their purposes were to be happy, to have a rest from being pressured
about achievement, and therefore to do just enough studying to
'get by'. Such students showed resistance to official indicators of
success, frequently missing classes and failing to complete home-
work. Some also resisted Florence's inclusive attempts to develop a
rapport with them, which she hoped would enable her to understand obstacles to their learning and engage them more effectively.
Despite these difficulties, and largely through the deliberate actions
of the tutor, the AS French site became increasingly synergistic
through the year.

However, things were to change in the second year of our fieldwork. The college was then going through a funding crisis, which
closely followed a major staffing reorganisation, which Florence
had already found stressful. She found herself working for a new
manager, who did not know her work, and was not a MFL specialist.

Also, recruitment – although average for the course – was below the new minimum class size stipulated by the college, and the immediate college reaction was to close the course. Florence fought hard to retain the course, but at a high cost. Contact time with students was cut from six hours per week to three, making it very difficult to get through the demanding syllabus, and support all the students in both language performance and written work. Moreover, the college decided to concentrate A2 provision in the three-hour evening class aimed mainly at part-time adults, making progression difficult for younger full-time students. Florence decided to leave, feeling forced out by the pressures of the new college situation (for a fuller account, see Colley et al. 2007). Thus, for the final year, there were deep tensions between the wider college culture and imperatives and both Florence's and the students' dispositions, as well as between the demands of the external examination and the low contact time.

When the learning cultures of the AS Psychology and AS French sites are compared, significant similarities and differences can be seen. Perhaps the main shared features derive from the nature of high-level academic work. Both courses had significant amounts of content to get through, and students had to achieve a high level of mastery in nine months. As well as bringing work pressure, this brought a fairly high element of risk for the students, because success was far from certain. Because of this, and of the high status of the courses, the impact on student dispositions was very varied. There was an initial buzz of anticipation and satisfaction from being accepted in the first place. For those who did well, this was further reinforced and intensified, as their self-esteem and confidence rose. However, for some who struggled, the opposite outcome was common – a progressive lowering of self-confidence, at least in relation to studying this subject at this level. In both groups there was a wide level of starting achievement. In the case of psychology, this was partly due to the recruitment policy, and the popularity of the subject. However, in both cases it was also influenced by the introduction of the one-year AS provision. This meant that some students who would not have enrolled for a two-year course happily signed up.

Differences were also important. On a national level psychology is a high-status subject, attracting large numbers of students. By contrast, only small numbers pursue any foreign language at AS/A2 level. There is a cultural resistance in Britain to learning other languages, and this situation was compounded by a government decision to remove MFL as a compulsory subject at Key Stage 4 in schools during the time of our research. Also the subject matter itself was different. While psychology can be characterised as primarily concerned about learning and understanding propositional knowledge, the French course entailed language performance. Sharing in this performance of language regularly helped integrate the group, and helped the tutor understand different student needs. The student intakes were also different. In psychology there were twenty-nine students, comprising school leavers and mature adults most of whom had no prior experience of the subject. On the French course, there was a smaller group of mainly young women, studying full-time, and all of whom had at least some prior language ability. Another key difference was contact time. For the first year in which we studied the site, AS French had six hours' contact time, with additional language support and access to a language lab. Psychology had three hours. Both tutors were charismatic and highly effective, but Florence was more concerned and able to engage with every single student – to know them, and react differently to their needs. She was aided in this by the longer contact time and the smaller student group. As a result of all these things, the French group became cohesive and closely knit – further aided by the tutor's identification with the students as rebels. The psychology class split into distinctive subgroups, whose dispositions towards the course, whose activities on it, and whose learning from it differed quite sharply. It was for these reasons that AS French was much more synergistic than AS Psychology – though, as we have seen, that synergy was fragile, and was seriously undermined in the second year of the research.

Conclusion: why learning cultures are important

In the previous section we had space to compare the learning cultures in two groups of learning sites. However, the approach would have been equally illuminating for other less obvious combinations. We have written briefly elsewhere (Hodkinson et al. 2004) about the value of comparing learning cultures for sites engaged with the least able learners, and of doing the same for what might be termed more ephemeral sites. These were sites where provision was recently developed to meet particular student needs, often through the drive and initiative of one tutor, and often in response to some new European or UK government initiative.

The findings from the TLC project suggest that using a learning cultures approach to understanding and improving learning is valuable at different scales of focus. As we saw in Chapter 3, the approach can be applied to a whole sector, such as FE, when it helps reveal common features which are often taken for granted. It also works for groups of learning sites, as we have just seen. Among other things, it then helps to distinguish between characteristics that are common for that type of site, from those that are site specific. It also works at the level of a single learning site.

At whatever scale the approach is used, some key benefits result, and some of the main ones are listed below:

- It shows how complex interrelationships influence learning.
- It shows that both external and internal factors influence learning in any site.
- It enables a clearer identification of any barriers to effective learning, as well as synergies that promote it.
- It shows more clearly what can be achieved to preserve and enhance effective learning, and who might action those changes.
- It makes clear the extent to which learning effectiveness lies within or beyond the scope of a particular tutor or teaching team.
- It raises awareness of possibly undesirable learning, and facilitates considered judgements about the value of learning, as well as its effectiveness.

Later in the book (Chapter 6), the issue of improving learning will be addressed more specifically, and in more detail. Here, we conclude by restating our major claim. On balance, learning will be more effective if the synergy between different factors influencing learning can be increased. However, it does not necessarily follow that learning which is more effective is also of greater value or even more appropriate. Synergy always brings a down-side, and the secret of enhancing learning is to balance judgements of value with judgements of effectiveness.

Notes

1 This chapter builds upon substantial contributions from Graham Anderson, Helen Colley, Jennie Davies, Kim Diment, Denis Gleeson, David James, Tony Scaife, Michael Tedder, Madeleine Wahlberg and Eunice Wheeler.
2 This was the spur to members of the team developing innovative data-gathering methods that utilised drama as a research tool (see, for example, Diment 2005).

Chapter 5

The learning of practices and the practices of learning

Introduction

Earlier in this book we noted the sheer diversity of provision contained within Further Education colleges. Some of this variation is clearly visible, even to a casual observer. For example, there are different subjects or disciplines, and some courses have a clear vocational identity, while others do not. Or again, some courses are full-time, some part-time, and some in-between, and they may be organised to include face-to-face and/or virtual contact, and activities may be group-based and/or individual. There are however other important ways in which provision may differ but which are harder to appreciate, even if they are clearly labelled. These include the 'level' of the provision ('entry level', 'level 3' etc.), and the meaning of assessment tasks and criteria. Furthermore, there are features of learning sites that do not reveal themselves at all on a day-to-day basis, or are so much part of a taken-for-granted reality that they do not usually attract any notice or comment. Our research suggests that Further Education colleges not only contain a wide range of different learning sites, but also encompass a range of different *cultures*, and that inside each of these there is often a strong sense of 'the way things are and have to be'.

Learning cultures differ in how, and how much, they affect the people within them. At the same time, they differ in how, and how much, the people within them can and do change the culture. The main purpose of this chapter is to focus on the first of these, that is, on some of the ways in which people are changed by virtue of being part of a learning culture in Further Education. As with other parts of the book, we are not attempting to provide a comprehensive account of the all the ways in

Authored by David James, Jennie Davies and Gert Biesta

which this can happen. Rather, we are illustrating some of the ways in which it *does* happen, on the grounds that the understanding this generates is useful and can provide insights that can be taken into other settings.

There are two principal ways in which the TLC project's data and analysis can illuminate the question of how learning cultures change people, and this chapter deals with each in turn. The first is to look at *the learning of practices*, that is, the kinds of change, shaping, development or socialisation that people undergo in a learning culture. This encompasses the smallest through to the biggest of changes and includes learning to be something or someone, and learning to become something or someone. Our consideration of it includes teasing out some of the differences between learning cultures. Second, we look at *the practices of learning*. Here, we explore examples of what definitions of learning prevail and are enacted in different learning cultures, once again illustrating differences and trying to show something of the range and variety in what sorts of learning are promoted, permitted, inhibited or ruled out. However, it is worth saying that the separation of these two approaches is something of a device to help with clarity of explanation: the 'learning of practices' and the 'practices of learning' are always closely related.

The learning of practices

The learning cultures we studied differed on a number of key dimensions. They were:

- more or less *immersing* for the people within them
- more or less *intentional* in their *attempts to change* the people within them
- more or less *attuned to a specific vocational field*
- more or less *expansive* in terms of progression
- more or less *transforming* for the people within them.

These dimensions are briefly illustrated in the following discussion of some of the learning sites in the project.

The CACHE site gave us our strongest example of a highly immersing and specifically socialising culture. The course included both college-based work and practical placements in schools and nurseries. It was a place where young women learned to become 'the right person for the job' of nursery nursing and were marginalised or left the course if, for some reason, they failed to achieve this.[1] We developed the notion of 'vocational habitus' to help explain this process, since much of what the students learned to do was to orient to an idealised set of dispositions for the 'good nursery nurse' promoted in their college course and to a different set of dispositions demanded by the workplace (Colley et al. 2003b). Orienting to this vocational habitus of a nursery nurse involved some academic work though in the main it was a practice-oriented course with a range of skills and knowledge. It also involved learning to manage their own emotional reactions and those of the children in their care, and contained a series of opportunities for students to display a strong notion of what it meant to behave 'professionally' in ways that would inspire confidence in their moral propriety among the parents of the children (see also Skeggs 1997). It involved students coming to accept low pay and a subordinate position in relation to other professional groups such as teachers and health workers. The 'nice' persona of the rounded and successful nursery nurse was one in which patience and self-control had been thoroughly incorporated (see Colley 2006; Colley et al. 2003b).

The CACHE course was at level 3 and, technically, students can progress to higher-level study having completed it. In practice, however, such progression was very rare, and on the whole students went into employment as nursery nurses. This was in contrast to the Health Studies BTEC course, also at level 3. Here, young female students followed a programme that was more academically oriented than the Child Care one, and although there were practice-based placements, these had a lower importance in the assessment regime. In this site, the career ambitions of young people expanded and became more diffuse over time, and included various routes of progression including to Higher Education. Tutors saw their role as broadening student horizons beyond the more 'obvious' career choices such as nursing (Tedder 2002; Colley et al. 2003b).

As well as being conceived at the same level of study (level 3), these two vocational courses also overlapped in terms of subject matter (placements in the area of child care were one of three types available to students on the Health Studies BTEC). Yet the sites are poles apart in terms of the relationship they had with the world of work. Where one was a specific vocational preparation which embodied and was defined by the values and expectations of the occupation itself, the other was a general vocational programme with more of a 'college' identity and which contained a process of *sampling* relevant workplaces. It is this *cultural* difference, more than anything else, which gave the conditions

for the distinctive educational experiences that these courses offered
to students, and which framed what counted as learning and achievement, or good and bad teaching (and therefore, improvement) in each
setting.[2]

Of course, the comparison just made mentions only two of a range of
possible relationships that might pertain between a learning culture
and a vocational culture. Another variant is that represented by another
of the learning sites we looked at, also at level 3, namely a course leading to a National Certificate in Electronics and Telecommunications
Engineering. This course was run as a day-release programme over two
years in a series of agreements with employers. All but one of the
students were male. Students and tutors were unanimous in their
descriptions of (and complaints about) a great distance between the
content of the course and the knowledge and skills that were being
practised and developed by the students for the rest of the week in their
workplaces. Tutors attributed this 'vocational irrelevance' to the examining board being out of touch or using inappropriate industry advisers,
though they also acknowledged that both the breadth of knowledge
and the pace of change in the relevant industries would make it difficult
to write any curriculum specification that would suit everyone.

Of all the recurrent themes in policy debates in post-compulsory
education and training, the degree of vocational relevance of the
curriculum, and the implications of this for national prosperity, must be
the most persistent. The most celebrated moment in this ongoing debate
must be James Callaghan's Ruskin College speech in October 1976, but
a perceived disconnection between education/training and the needs
of employers was also the major justification for the overhaul of vocational qualifications from the late 1980s and the establishment of NVQs,
and remains pivotal in contemporary policy (see, for example, Payne
1999; Foster 2005; DfES 2006). Yet within the learning culture of the
Electronic and Telecommunications Engineering learning site, we were
struck by the *acceptance* of 'vocational irrelevance' as 'the way things
are'. It appeared to present no threat to the high regard in which the
qualification continued to be held. The National Certificate had a long-
standing currency in the workplace, being seen as a genuine aid to the
occupational security, mobility and progression of those who managed
to complete it. Indeed, the endurance of irrelevance, which is also a
type of emotional management, seemed to be a central element of the
vocational habitus of this course, though in a masculinised form. At the
same time, unlike the child care and healthcare students, these students
felt like they had already become engineers, having been immersed in

the workplace culture for some time prior to starting the college course. It is no surprise, then, that the course was regarded very instrumentally by most students, as a rite of passage or something to be endured and overcome for career purposes (see Colley et al. 2003b and the discussion in Chapter 4).

This example illustrates how a course can be highly integrated with a vocational culture in all sorts of respects while at the same time retaining a separate curricular identity from the workplace. Organisationally, day-release modes of operation require a high level of contact and negotiation with employers. In the context of a rapidly changing industry which was in some respects declining, the very existence of the National Certificate programme was determined directly by a small group of employers. Towards the end of our fieldwork, and following many years of declining demand for this and other engineering courses, there was a strong expectation that this course would close. In the event it continued in a limited form, because a new employer client was found who wanted students to complete the qualification in the space of one year instead of the customary two. Tutors rapidly redesigned the course as a one-year part-time programme, though saw this compression process as a high-risk strategy. Nevertheless, they saw it as 'necessary for the survival of the National Certificate'. Here, then, the nature of the student (and tutor) experience of a programme of study is framed by a new settlement between the interests of an employer and those of the college and some of its staff, but one in which elements of traditional, established practices remain important. This learning site illustrates how a learning culture can be highly attuned and responsive to a vocational field, while at the same time what is actually taught, learnt and assessed is perceived by all the immediate participants as showing *disconnection* between the two.

The three examples mentioned so far give us a glimpse of three very different possibilities in the way that a vocational field can be related to the learning of practices within a course in a Further Education college. This is important, given that the nature and quality of learning and teaching is usually thought to be (mainly or exclusively) a function of tutors and students and how they interact. Occupations and professions usually have a 'vocational culture' (Bates 1994) or a prevailing ideology of practice (N. James 1989):

> In caring occupations, for example, the prevailing ideology is one of 'sacrificial femininity' . . . linked to affect (the construction, management and display of feelings) and moral rectitude (appearing

'nice', being 'nice' and 'doing good'). . . . The vocational culture of engineering reflects the other side of the male-female, rational-emotional hierarchy that prevails in patriarchal capitalist society. It privileges logical thinking, technological invention, and judgement divorced from the 'human side' of problems. . . . It also encourages an instrumental approach to studying.

(Colley et al. 2003b: 488)

It is common to regard discussions like the foregoing as being about 'context' rather than about 'learning itself'. However, the approach adopted by the TLC project highlights why such vocational cultures cannot be regarded as merely part of the backdrop against which tutors and students get on with the presumed-to-be 'neutral' activities of teaching, learning and assessment. Rather, vocational cultures are sometimes highly defining of the learning culture, depending on a number of historical and contemporary circumstances. As in the examples discussed, expectations to do with social class and gender are often deeply rooted in learning cultures, though it would be wrong to suggest that vocational cultures are always a dominant or unidirectional influence in this regard. The general point illustrates why it can take much more than an innovative and energetic tutor, or a glossy prospectus with photographs of girls becoming engineers, to change the nature of a learning culture.

For many tutors and managers in Further Education colleges, proximity to a vocational culture is something to be nurtured and exploited. Student placements, such as those already mentioned in the CACHE and the Health Studies BTEC courses, are a common method of gaining such proximity. Other ways in which this can be realised include: a teacher inviting an experienced practitioner to visit and talk or demonstrate something; a student trip to a relevant plant or workplace; an assessed task that requires students to look at the *application* of an idea or design. For many college-based courses, such activities do more than demonstrate the 'relevance' of the provision. They enhance its credibility, and may have pay-offs in terms of the employability and progression for students.

Some colleges and tutors go to considerable lengths in attempting to build up elements of a vocational culture in a course. A good example of this (though one with unexpected consequences) arose during the period of the project fieldwork in a collection of courses in the Photography learning site. Here, Paul and his colleagues ran a programme with three different qualification outcomes. Triggered in part by a wish to be more efficient, the tutors worked together to set up a regime that simulated the vocational situation of many professional photographers. Students would come in at agreed times for group and individual activities, including setting up projects and opportunities for collective evaluation of work. At other times they would drop in as and when they needed to use the darkroom and other facilities, or see a tutor in addition to scheduled arrangements. Tutors and students, on the whole, regarded this new arrangement as successful, both in terms of the efficient use of resources and in the way it modelled the work pattern and mode of operation of many photographers. However, during an audit process, the tutors were criticised for not having adequate records of regular student attendance, and with the threat of a loss of funding, the learning site immediately reverted to a traditional timetabled arrangement and conventional attendance registers. This had a very negative impact on tutor and student morale, but the issues of most relevance here are, first, that staff themselves attempted to change the nature of the learning activities in quite a radical way to bring them closer to the vocational culture, in one sense compensating for the absence of a unified vocational 'voice',[3] and second, that this attempt failed in the face of college and sector 'quality' systems which brought with them other strong definitions of learning and teaching, which in this instance had a greater power to define the curriculum and the pedagogy.

Learning cultures can be more or less shaped and defined by the expectations of the vocational field, and naturally this affects what students do and how they are changed in a learning process. An important part of a learning culture is that it has some boundaries, and that it 'rules in' and 'rules out' certain definitions of learning. We return to this point in the second half of this chapter. But before leaving aside the discussion about the various influences of the vocational culture, there is a further important point to be made. It is that the influences are not simply unidirectional, with the vocational culture shaping the learning culture. At the same time, the learning culture will have more or less synergy with the vocational culture, feeding and strengthening some aspects of it, and, potentially, detracting from and weakening others. An example here would be the way that, despite some conscious efforts in the respective colleges, both the Child Care Education and the National Certificate in Electronics and Telecommunications Engineering learning sites continued to 'reproduce' the highly gendered, traditional recruitment practices in each vocational field. It is crucial to consider the impact this has on what is learnt and not learnt, and perhaps also worth considering the various costs and benefits to all parties involved (students, college, employers, tutors) if this pattern were to be disrupted.

We also suggest that ideas like 'reproduction' never sum up all that is going on in a learning culture. Even in the most vocationally oriented course, it would be wrong to see students as merely acquiring or taking on board whole sets of practices, norms and beliefs that come to them from a vocational culture: reality is more complex than that. For one thing, there is an interaction between the dispositions of the student and the learning culture: a student can find themselves anywhere on a continuum from 'like a fish in water' through to 'completely alienated', depending upon how their dispositions play out in the learning culture. This complexity requires that we use concepts such as orientation and that we appreciate the interaction of 'realised' and 'idealised' identities in trying to capture the dynamic process of, for example, 'becoming a nursery nurse' (see Colley et al. 2003b: 487–493).

Learning cultures may be stronger or weaker in terms of how they attempt to socialise people, but it is a separate and more complex question as to whether, and in what senses, they might *transform* people (or provide a means for people to transform) in some meaningful and recognisable sense. It is clear that the CACHE site, mentioned in the earlier discussion, offers strong socialisation and is also highly transforming, if in a specific direction. In this respect, it has similarities with a significant amount of vocational provision across the FE sector. What is less immediately apparent would be its similarities with some examples of more 'academic' study. In the AS French site a particular combination of the tutor's values and pedagogy meant that there was extensive use of the target language in the teaching sessions. This added up to a highly structured learning experience that was quite deeply (and intentionally) socialising and which also transformed students, powerfully so in the case of some of those whose backgrounds – and specifically, an absence of foreign holidays – would not otherwise have brought them into direct contact with the target language.

Yet other learning cultures appeared to contain claims or intentions about the socialisation of students, but were not much characterised by students undergoing personal transformation. Indeed, in some sites 'transformation' was not a term that could be applied to the vast majority of students, and students were engaged in activities that appeared to maintain the status quo in respect of their capacities and relationships with others. Examples of this would be two of the courses aimed at students with special needs, namely the Entry Level Drama and Connect

2, another entry level course for school leavers with moderate learning and behavioural difficulties. In the first of these, and as we say in Chapter 4, the learning culture was one we characterised as 'a family'. The tutor was committed to providing a safe haven for students who needed continuity, security and support. Routine and repetition – for example using certain drama exercises in a group setting – were seen as more valuable to students' well-being than things which would present them with new challenges and which could therefore disrupt a familiar cycle of activity. Avoiding risks to vulnerable students was also a factor in what the tutor chose to do, or not do, with the students. While it was very difficult to achieve any reliable information about student expectations in this site it was clear that parents and the tutor were content with how things were running. The site appeared to represent a successful learning culture, but one that was characterised by forms of participation that were difficult to recognise and record in conventional college systems. A case in point would be the idea of 'progression'. Like the concept of 'level', on which it depends, 'progression' can be very convincing in theory while being highly problematic in practice. In Entry Level Drama and in other sites we studied, tutors expressed a great deal of frustration with college systems that did not (or could not) recognise many of the learning outcomes they knew had been achieved by students. These outcomes, which included raised confidence, greater self-determination and the capacity to make better judgements, could not always be translated into conventionally recognised qualifications, measurements of progression, or level. Thus, provision which might appear to reproduce the 'circuits of training' identified by Riddell and colleagues as 'a key weakness of existing provision' (Riddell et al. 2006) may have other outcomes that are, to some extent, 'below the radar'.

In Connect 2, there was some clear evidence of student personal transformation, such as the student who was in a process of rejecting her 'disabled' status, or the elective mute student who began to talk (so much that the tutor had to intervene to try to stop him from disturbing others' learning). A more general trend was that many students gained in confidence, by their own and their tutors' reckoning. However, in our analysis of this site, we distinguished between a public, 'sacred' story of onward progression, of acquiring ever more skills, of students moving ever closer towards a 'good job', and on the other hand a 'profane' story of students reaching a plateau and not moving into employment. A related course to Connect 2 provided a progression route for some students, but there was considerable ambiguity (for tutors as well as students) as to whether this other course was at a higher level, or simply had a different, more confident intake. Arguably, this ambiguity was itself functional for the group of staff concerned, because it helped them satisfy institutional demands about *demonstrating* progression and achievement. In this site, then, there were some clear instances of 'transformation', but they were again difficult to express in forms the wider college (and sector) would recognise, and our data suggests they were a few celebrated examples against a general backdrop of more modest changes. Yet no matter how dramatic or significant the individual cases, or how worthwhile or otherwise the provision is felt to be, both these sites illustrate a tension between certain *educational* models and contemporary college systems. In fact, this gap between the learning culture of the site and that of the college and sector makes such provision vulnerable. Shortly after the end of our fieldwork, the Entry Level Drama courses were being wound down on the grounds that they were uneconomic. Similarly, the teaching on Connect 2 was increasingly amalgamated with programmes such as Entry to Employment, which stressed the acquisition of specific knowledge and skills rather than the development of general self-confidence within a group of vulnerable students.

There were several other learning sites where the ostensible purposes of a course were highly socialising in a vocational direction, but the practices we observed and recorded suggested something else was happening. A good example of this was the Travel and Tourism site, with one and two-year routes leading to an Advanced Vocational Certificate of Education (AVCE). There was a marked lack of synergy between how the tutor and students saw the position and importance of the vocational element, and few students saw themselves going forward to work in the collection of occupations covered in the programme: for them, the course was more akin to a general education allowing various forms of progression. Recruitment processes had been problematic, with a number of concessions being made regarding prior student attainments so as to get sufficient students for a viable group. Many of the students struggled with the academic demands of the course, and several told us that their part-time jobs were more important to them than their studies. It seemed to us that despite the energy and enthusiasm of the tutor, this learning site suffered from a type of structural identity crisis. It appeared to be functioning as a 'general vocational' course, but also as a second-chance, and second-choice, academic general education. The students who did best in conventional terms were those whose previous academic achievements were relatively high, and there was no clear evidence of other kinds of trans-formation (as there was in some of the sites for students with special educational needs, for example). Recognising this raises uncomfortable questions about whether courses in this position are of net benefit to the students that follow them.

Our design allowed us to follow learning sites over a period of up to two years, and we were able to see how particular goals or objectives played out over time. This highlighted a series of intended and unin-tended consequences with regard to socialisation and transformation. In the Pathways for Parents site, a clear initial aim of the college had been to depathologise the social position of young mothers as well as to offer them a curriculum that would directly support them and which would, to some extent, respond to what they said they wanted most (which included first aid for babies; healthy eating; sewing and sign language). After this initial participatory phase, there was a radical shift to a curriculum that maximised the college's funding through a focus on level 2 certificated courses, particularly Basic Skills. This change had a negative impact on the students' sense of ownership of the course, though some students welcomed the certification, which opened up new avenues for the possibility of a career. There was, therefore, a shift around who was socialising whom – from the college being socialised by the young parents starting to 'normalise' the needs of young parents coming to college, to the young parents being socialised by the college.

In another of the learning sites, a crucial difference emerged between the explicit aims (which did not include an intention to change people) and the actual practices of tutor and learners (which did). This was the work-based NVQ Assessment site. Here, the students were officially candidates for assessment rather than 'students' as such, and they were located in a range of workplaces. The explicit purpose of their connec-tion with the college tutor was to be assessed against the competence statements within various National Vocational Qualifications (NVQs) at levels 2 and 3. However, the tutor concerned spent a great deal of time and energy supporting the 'candidates' in their learning, and this appeared to account for her very high pass rate, and for outcomes that, for many, had a genuine and positive impact on career progression. Yet her efforts of this kind were completely unresourced, unofficial and outside the tutor's job description. Our analysis suggests that her facilitation of learning was a product of her professional *habitus*, based on years of experience of what students needed in order to learn (and therefore, to succeed in assessment). Our case study of this situation shows how a particular form of competence-based assessment (the 'technology' of NVQs) asserts a fundamental distinction between *learning* and *assessment*, as if they could be treated separately. This separation was embedded in funding arrangements. But when these factors came together with the tutor's well-established professional disposition, the result was *underground teaching and underground learning* where the real work of teaching and learning and the reasons for its success were hidden from view (James and Diment 2003). Our evidence suggests that this is quite a widespread phenomenon in FE colleges.

Finally, it is worth noting that some FE provision has a learning culture that permits very broad, open-ended notions of learning and change, and individual students are expected to learn, develop or achieve in a wide variety of ways. An example would be the IT Skills 7261 site, which existed for the first year of our fieldwork, and for which there are many parallels in other colleges. The main reason for citing this is to point out that the purposes of provision in Further Education are just too broad and diverse to make any blanket normative judgements (such as the judgement that transformation is generally a good thing). This particular learning site was conceived and operated as a service that could be accessed by individual students as and when – and only as much as – they thought they needed it. This decision sometimes involved the advice of tutors in other parts of the college. For some students, contact with such a service could be transforming in a fundamental sense (learning to word-process for the first time, or to use the internet to find things out, for example). This particular learning site changed in a fundamental way after one year, becoming part of a fully certificated provision that had the effect of removing the 'open-ended' aspect.

The practices of learning

So far in this chapter we have considered some of the main ways in which learning cultures can differ, some of the reasons for this, and also some of the effects in terms of the learning of practices. This brings us to a second, related question. What form does *learning* take in different learning cultures?

Chapter 2 set out how the TLC project developed a *theory of learning cultures* and a *cultural theory of learning*. An important element of the first of these is that learning cultures are not just 'contexts' or 'containers', but are made up of the social practices through which people learn. This, in turn, means that it is very important to gain some appreciation of how learning cultures differ. What do they allow, disallow, encourage or discourage in the name of learning, and why? Do such differences seem to matter? We start with two 'vignettes' taken from our case study of English for Speakers of Other Languages learning site.

Vignette 1

The tutor Ruth told a story about one of her students, called Mohamed. Like many of her students, Mohamed was an asylum seeker. However, he was younger than most, at just 16 years old, and had arrived in England unaccompanied by a parent or carer, and was being looked after by Social Services. After making some progress in a small literacy-focused ESOL class, Mohamed joined a larger ESOL group with a broader curriculum, which the tutor described as 'well-established, lively and friendly'. However, Mohamed seemed withdrawn and unwilling to get involved and soon his attendance and punctuality worsened. Ruth met him for a one-to-one tutorial and pointed out that she was expected to inform the social worker about his non-attendance, and that this could affect the benefit payments he was receiving. With hindsight, Ruth thought Mohamed had found the larger ESOL group rather intimidating and she reflected upon the limited opportunities he would have had to act as an independent adult prior to joining her class. However, the story ends on a more positive note, because within just a few months, the curriculum of the ESOL group had developed more of a focus on literacy, making Mohamed one of the more skilled members of the group. As Ruth put it:

> He is now a confident, cheerful young man in the classroom and is making steady progress – not the highest praise I have ever given a student but a huge improvement for him and one that will enable him to improve his English and build himself a life in this country.

Vignette 2

Khalida, another of Ruth's students, had come to England from Pakistan while in her early twenties, and had worked for a relative in a factory where not much English was spoken. She then married a

continued

man from Pakistan, and moved to a new city, but rapidly became isolated, having left behind her friends and finding she had to rely on her husband and his family in any situation requiring the use of English. Khalida joined a beginner's ESOL class and then attended a workshop programme for nearly two years. The workshop programme was a planned but flexible series of sessions which allowed students to find a balance with other commitments and to make progress at their own pace.

Khalida's contact with the ESOL provision was a transforming experience, giving her the tools and confidence for independent travel (so she could visit her friends once again) and enabling her to form new friendships in her new location. Khalida telephoned Emergency Services for an ambulance when her father-in-law collapsed and this probably saved his life: she could not have done the same two years earlier.

There are strong clues here about how learning is defined and practised by Ruth and many of her colleagues. Some of our project interviews and meetings focused on what tutors and students defined as 'high quality learning', and Ruth explained a little further why she chose the example of Mohamed in particular:

> You . . . may find it surprising that I offer this story as an example of high quality learning when most of my other students have progressed further academically and more quickly. When thinking about this question I asked myself, 'Who am I most impressed with and proud of at the moment?', and an image of Mohamed achieving and looking pleased with himself rose before my eyes. I think this reveals something about my motivation as a teacher; I take great delight in seeing progress for the students who start off struggling. I am also as interested in my students' disposition and outlook on life as I am in their academic achievement. Mohamed is now 17 and though he still needs to improve his study skills, the changes he has already made make it possible for him to improve his English, progress to other vocational or academic courses, and to get and keep a job. As a basic skills tutor, what more can I ask?

Ruth's way of conceiving *learning* appears to encompass ideas like 'distance travelled' as much as 'level reached'. She is also concerned with more than the particular achievements in terms of the curriculum, paying as much attention to the impact of participation on the lives of those she teaches. Furthermore, Ruth is concerned with her own learning, in that this episode caused her to look at her own assumptions and to reach a different understanding. For example, she reflected upon the limitations of how she had tried at first to deal with Mohamed's attendance and punctuality, and at how she had mistakenly assumed that he was just as much an 'independent adult' as the rest of her students. From the following academic year, the proportion of young people actually increased in Ruth's ESOL groups, and she saw her experience with Mohamed as an important preparation for this shift.

As we grew more familiar with this learning site and compared data from student and tutor interviews, observations, the tutor's diary and between-tutor shadowing, it became clear that here, *learning* was *primarily* to do with the empowerment of individuals in a range of situations and relationships, most of them ordinary and everyday. Ruth and her colleagues are intervening to change sets of circumstances which, if left as they were, would continue to deny the people concerned some of the scope they could have to be self-determining in the most practical of senses. It would be a mistake to bracket this off as 'motivational factors', and therefore part of 'context' or 'background' for learning. Students were putting their everyday experiences on the table, as it were, and these were the starting-point for learning. The tools or means to bring about learning (such as specific activities and assessments to do with vocabulary, grammar and language usage, etc.), for all their importance, do not sum up *learning* in this site. It is significant that Ruth and some of her colleagues find Paolo Friere's writing helpful in reflecting upon, theorising and improving their professional practice. One of the central tenets of such writing is that educational processes are never neutral, but act to *either* empower *or* to disempower the learners (see, for example, Freire 1972; Taylor 1993).

The discussion above is an illustration of how a cultural theory of learning can illuminate practice in ways that take us beyond conventional views. Our investigations in other learning sites revealed other important departures from common assumptions about learning. The Photography site, among others, challenges the idea that learning is always really an individual matter. The *learning of the group* and the *learning of individuals* were two overlapping but different and important considerations for both students and tutors. Under the first come such matters as students learning to work together; the collective capacity to produce and judge items of work along technical, aesthetic and conceptual lines; the development of the collective capacity for the students to discuss their own and each others' work (and that of other photographers) and to offer constructive criticism in terms that more experienced practitioners would recognise. Under the second, the tutor and his colleagues recognised that their students differed a great deal, and that while many were interested in acquiring a level of knowledge and competence in the area of photography, there were others with higher expectations, for whom becoming a photographer was more of a fundamental issue of passion and vocation. This meant the student finding and developing a distinctive 'voice' or style as a photographer. Thus, staff were adapting to different individual dispositions, purposes and potential. They went to some trouble to support students whose work and efforts appeared promising in this respect, seeing the provision as a platform that could nurture some individuals in more specific ways and enable them to move beyond the limits of staff expertise and knowledge to connect with key figures in the wider community of practice. But for all students, learning was conceived and practiced as both a shared *and* an individual entity here, while in some other sites it was located more with the individual, even if some of the means to make it happen were collective.

One of the most widely held distinctions in teaching and learning practices, in FE but also in HE and schools, is that between 'transmission' and 'student-centred' approaches. These terms sometimes refer to whole theoretical edifices, or to traditionalism versus progressivism in pedagogy and curriculum. However, a simpler version of the distinction is usually voiced by tutors, students and managers. In many learning sites, it was common to see a combination of activities that could be crudely classified as either 'the acquiring of information' or as 'engagement in activity'. Tutors often had a carefully considered rationale for how they had chosen and combined elements of these two categories, and providing students with 'variety' was a frequent wish. A few tutors called upon theories when explaining how they had designed and organised sessions with students. Examples included a dictum commonly attributed to Lao Tsu or Confucius,[4] the work of humanist educators such as Carl Rogers, and the learning theory of D.A. Kolb (whose *experiential learning cycle* presents a rationale for 'designing in' such things as *concrete experience* and *active experimentation*). Kolb's theory has also produced one of the most influential and widespread approaches to measuring 'learning styles'. The popularity and usage of learning styles questionnaires far outstrips the evidence base, probably because there is a high expectation that colleges and other providers demonstrate that they are striving to meet the needs of individual learners (see Coffield et al. 2004).

In the Health Studies BTEC course, students particularly enjoyed – and claimed to learn most from – those sessions that were highly participative. Typically, students would have to solve a problem using some informational resources and each other, or carry out a practical experiment to highlight key aspects of a topic in the curriculum. A typical example was a 'taste and touch experiment' in which students simulated various sensory impairments. In another, they swabbed parts of the room and each other to investigate the incidence and distribution of microbes. With the 'taste and touch' experiment, Gill, the tutor, was very pleased that students had developed a strong appreciation of how vulnerable they felt as they role-played people with a significant sensory impairment. She felt that this empathy was itself motivating for the students, and decided to use it as a jumping-off point in further sessions that were more information driven. Like many courses across Further Education, though by no means all, tutors here had constantly to make judgements about if, when and how to 'design in' such activity. They decided what sort of balance to strike between structured activity and parts of sessions given over to information-giving, assessment tasks, tutorial support, independent study or other ways of working. They took into account many different factors in these decisions, including student backgrounds and expectations, the amount of material to be covered in a given timescale, and whether there was close scrutiny and negative consequences if they failed to 'cover the syllabus' in the time allocated.

In the example above, Gill's teaching approach would be widely regarded as 'good practice'. However, a cultural perspective on this tutor's situation adds a further, crucial dimension to our understanding. Gill's decisions are framed not only by her values and pedagogic theories or approaches, but also by the *positioning* of the course, which, like the Travel and Tourism one, is located between two dominant discourses that give both academic and vocational routes a clearer identity. One of the goals in both courses is to 'broaden horizons' and to encourage students to consider options beyond the 'obvious' ones. This gives a legitimate space for curricula and pedagogic exploration, and makes such exploration appear less risky than it would seem in (say) AS Psychology, Electronic and Telecommunications Engineering or in CACHE. In sum, the learning culture here is partly defined by an ambiguity of purpose and a freedom from the immediate necessities of many academic and vocational courses. This gives the tutor and students a certain kind of freedom for *educational* work, but any serious attempt to evaluate the provision would have to take into account prior student dispositions and a longer view of what students end up doing. At best, the learning in this site could be an expansive, critical and creative process that leaves the students with a recognised qualification, better self-knowledge and some understanding and capacities that enable them to engage more intelligently with the Healthcare sector, or to move away from it for good reasons. At worst, it could be an ill-defined general education that confirms social location,[5] with lower entrance requirements and lower status than established academic routes. It may also be an individually costly postponement of decision-making in relation to a vocational area.

For many years it has been common for staff development in the area of teaching and learning to offer various 'recipes' for the enhancement of quality. The way that these change over time gives them the appearance of 'fashions' in the eyes of some tutors. But what most of the 'recipes' have in common is a technocratic view of teaching and learning, in which, once it has been identified, good practice is infinitely transferable. What the cultural approach shows us is that learning cultures frame what counts as learning, or good learning; that tutors are not on their own when they make decisions about what will happen in their learning site. In some sites, there were constraints upon both tutors and students that could severely limit their room for manoeuvre as definers of what counted as learning. An example of this in the project would be the Electrical Engineering National Certificate course discussed earlier in this chapter. Here, employer requirements, student expectations, a pressurised day-release mode of provision and a dense, highly structured, content-driven curriculum that was sometimes changed from on high at short notice, all left tutors little scope for anything except prescribed lectures, demonstrations and assessment. A different example of such constraints would be the AS French site, where the tutor's long-established and successful pedagogic style included extensive use of the target language. Yet as the college reduced the funding for this course, the tutor was asked to teach the same course in fewer and fewer hours per week. Eventually she decided that this was unsustainable, and this was a major factor in her leaving the college for other employment. As far as we could tell, there was no collective organisational learning from this incident.

Many of our interviews with students demonstrated the continuing importance of learning about educational provision and qualifications as *positional*, that is, forming a view of one's place in relation to other courses, qualifications, subjects, groups of people and so on. We have already touched upon this idea in relation to two general vocational courses which are seen by many as a second-best alternative to academic routes. Several electronic engineering students described in some detail how their current study represented a new direction after they had failed to complete other, more academic courses that had been their 'first choice'. Both students and tutors in much of the general vocational provision were troubled by issues of declared equivalence to A level academic qualifications, and some felt that their lower entry requirements and lower general recognition in the public eye gave them lower status than those academic courses. There were other kinds of positioning too: some female students spoke in terms of 'the scary parts of the college' and the 'non-girl territory' when referring to an engineering department. The general point arising from these examples is that a learning site and a learning culture do not exist in isolation from other sites and cultures, but are *partially defined* in relation to them, in a field of positions. Furthermore, an appreciation of a 'position' is often an important part of what the students actually learn, for better or worse.

Conclusion

Learning cultures are more than the sum of the parts. They also encompass a range of elements that are beyond the obvious physical boundaries of a learning site. They stretch beyond the apparent *temporal* boundaries too, in that a learning culture is usually there before a particular group of individuals arrive together, and usually continues after they have left. In this chapter we have been centrally concerned with two different angles from which we can shine a light on the process of learning cultures changing people. The first, termed *the learning of practices*, drew attention to a range of ways in which learning sites socialise and/or transform people – especially, but of course not only – students. The second, which we dubbed *the practices of learning*, addressed some examples of how different learning cultures can encourage, permit, discourage or prevent certain definitions and practices of learning.

But why does this matter? There are many answers to that question. The main one is that our data and approach presents a challenge to many common-sense and officially sanctioned assumptions and actions in relation to teaching and learning in Further Education. An examination and comparison of learning cultures questions the idea that teaching and learning (and particularly, good teaching and learning) is fundamentally the same process wherever it is found, and the related idea that 'good practice' is infinitely transferable. It challenges the notion that the individual teacher is *always* the prime determinant of the quality of learning, or the only one that really matters. It also shows up as problematic the idea that learning is something that is successfully codified into sets of learning outcomes and qualifications, and the assumption that these are what matters most to all those involved. Most of all, the approach challenges the common assumption that learning is largely a cognitive, individual process that just happens to be located in a context of some kind. We would argue that this last assumption is one that makes it particularly hard to see the inequality work that goes on in the name of learning, which is of course not confined to Further Education but is made especially visible there because of the juxtaposition of such a broad range of purposes and processes.

Notes

1 There was one young man and one mature female student among the students in this site. All the rest were young women.
2 It is also possible to see these two courses as occupying the lower and middle positions respectively on a tripartite hierarchy of (1) academic, (2) general vocational and (3) specific vocational routes.
3 Reflecting the dispersed nature of that professional group: photographers tend to be freelance or to work for very small organisations.
4 The dictum is 'I see and forget, I hear and remember, I do and I understand'. This has been a popular touchstone of FE pedagogic staff development.
5 In an article drawing upon case studies of the Travel and Tourism site and the Healthcare site, Davies and Tedder (2003) point out that most students came from families with little FE or HE. They also point to the physical location of these courses, away from the 'College Sixth Form Centre' which housed academic A level programmes (Davies and Tedder 2003: 521).

Chapter 6

Changing the culture
Interventions and mediations

Introduction

In the chapters so far we have shown what learning cultures are and how students learn as a result of their participation in learning cultures. In this chapter we focus on a question which, in a sense, is the most important question of the whole book, namely the question of *improvement*.[1] What is it that people can and cannot do to bring about change in a learning culture, and what helps them to judge whether it is change for the better? To explore this question we have to look at the ways in which key players involved try to *intervene* in learning cultures in order to bring about change. This is more difficult than it first appears, because in a sense tutors – and students – are 'intervening' in learning cultures all the time. So, for the purposes of this discussion, we need to think of *interventions* as the more pivotal moments in an ongoing process of *mediation*. We also have to recognise that improvement itself is not a straightforward idea: for example, something a tutor considers to be an improvement may not be seen as such by colleagues, college managers or even by students, and different yardsticks may be used by the different interests involved. Added to this, the various players differ in how much *power* they have to define 'improvement' and to make their definition 'stick'.

In this and the following chapter we try to unravel the complexities of change and improvement in teaching and learning in Further Education. In this chapter we focus primarily on the actions of tutors and, to some extent, on those of students and managers, while in Chapter 7 we ask what kind of professional it is possible to be in contemporary Further Education. We begin with some of the ideas about

Authored by David James, Madeleine Wahlberg and Gert Biesta

change that we found among the tutors and managers and we follow this with a pair of case stories. In each one a tutor develops a view that there is a need for something to change for the better, and engages in a conscious and deliberate sequence of actions to bring about that change. We use the two case stories as a springboard for a discussion of the TLC project's understanding of 'interventions'. We make a distinction between three types of intervention: interventions for improvement, interventions to mitigate negative change, and interventions for exit. We illustrate our discussion with examples of some of the intended and unintended consequences of interventions, and show how our cultural approach helped us to understand the complexities of changing learning cultures. The chapter then moves on to argue for a more useful notion of improvement, which grows from the combination of data analysis and theory. We conclude with a discussion of the opportunities for and limits of tutor intervention.

Understanding change and improvement

During the research we encountered several different ideas about how change and improvement can be brought about. First, there was what we could call the *technical* view of how change happens. Here, bringing about change was seen as a rational process of finding and building up knowledge about 'what works', communicating this to tutors in the form of recipes for action, and expecting that once tutors adopt these recipes, improvement will follow. Second, and in some ways opposite to this, many tutors seemed to hold a professional model of change. Central to this view is the idea of tutors who, based upon their knowledge and understanding and informed by their professional values and orientations, make judgements about the most appropriate course of action and, through acting upon their judgements, bring about change. A third view about change that we found among some tutors and managers sees change as closely connected to *market needs*. In this case tutors and managers need to find out what the market of students, employers or others wants and then change the college structures and teaching provision so as to provide this. The college should not try to judge whether the change is 'for the good', as the market will soon say if they have got it wrong. A fourth model that we have seen is focused on *power*. Change in the college happens, in this view, because managers are constantly manoeuvring in order to retain their power in a sea of shifting sands. The managers adopt the language of whatever idea is in fashion at the moment and use it in order to retain their position, and that of the college. If the *technical* model mentioned above is the one that many tutors felt *ought* to prevail, then the model based on power was the one that many of them felt *did in fact* prevail. Change in this model is thought to happen in a relatively chaotic way. Colleges are driven, mainly by central government, to continuous change, this way and that, without any real consideration of the implications, management and integrity of that change. There is not even much evaluation about what any one policy has achieved before further change is introduced.

We can see from this short discussion that tutors and managers in FE hold very different models both about how change does happen, and about how it ought to happen. Looking a bit harder at the first model as one example, although some of the tutors believed that this technical model was the ideal way to achieve change, as soon as anyone started to talk about this model, they burst its bubble, treating it as a fantasy. They would cite the reasons why it could not be carried out in a particular set of circumstances, or talk of it as an ideal situation for institutions changing policy – but not for professionals changing practice. One effect of this was to make this 'ideal' model of change unattainable, and the other models of change into second best, which undermined the practitioners as change-makers. Moreover, while at first sight, the technical model is attractive precisely because it appeals to common-sense logic and a clear, readily understandable sequence of events, there are lots of problems with it. To signal just three: first, it oversimplifies the social reality of a complex, dynamic activity; second, it assumes that teaching and learning are essentially the same everywhere; third, it usually seems to presume that it is *teachers and their teaching* that need improvement, when there are many other factors and issues involved. This reveals that it is not only the *content* of change that has implications for the power relations in FE, but also the *method* that is used, and how that is thought about. Models of change are not just value-free techniques. We will see some of this complexity in two examples – the stories of Joan and Rachel – which illustrate the challenge to some widely held ideas about the means to bring about improvement in teaching and learning.

Joan's story: 'getting to know you'

Joan worked in a large college of Further Education. She led a programme for students with moderate special educational needs. The unusual funding arrangements, and the special needs of these students, gave Joan considerable autonomy to decide on the most appropriate curriculum for these students. Moreover, as entry to this course did not rely on prior qualification levels, Joan needed some other way to choose the intake. Joan taught a course that focused on enhancing the self-esteem of these students and this required her to have very close knowledge of the students' individual needs.

As part of her involvement in the research, Joan chose an intervention – a deliberate attempt to bring about change – based on improving her knowledge of these students. Joan was aware that the schools, and increasingly the Connexions Service, already held a good deal of information on the students, and she was anxious to be able to put it to good use. It would help her to fit the student to a suitable course, and support the learning process in general. Joan devised a very formal plan for this intervention, drawing up eleven points for action against a time-line.

Joan chose this intervention as a relatively 'free' agent, and did not seem to be under any pressure to pursue it. However, it is worth noting that the circumstances favoured this kind of change, placing a new premium on knowledge about the individual needs and abilities of students. There were four key contextual factors, as follows:

- The majority of the students coming on to Joan's course had been through the statutory system for identifying special needs ('Statementing'). Detailed summative reports on each of these students were therefore available.
- Individualised learning: like many colleges, this college had placed the identification of individual learning needs at the centre of its strategy to improve learning and achievement. In the words of an assistant principal, 'I think that it is (now) inappropriate to talk of the generic needs of a particular group of students. The issue is the individual learning styles'. This focus on individual need was to be realised through changes to the interviewing process for would-be students; the use of a new standardised screening test for additional support; the use of a learning styles questionnaire; and a new stress on strategies for differentiated learning.
- Funding for Basic and Key Skills teaching: there was college-wide pressure to get students to undertake more level 1 and 2 skills courses, and thereby to attract more of these funds. This required the active search for 'failures' at numeracy and literacy so as to direct such students onto these courses.
- Changes in other services: in the new Connexions (career advice) Service, all personal advisers would now prepare reports on individual students in school Year 11, including special Learning

Difficulties and Disabilities (LDD) reports. Thus, summative reports already existed for these students.

It would appear that Joan's planned intervention was going with the flow of change in college and national policy. Nevertheless, Joan found it difficult to bring about change. She found it very difficult to get permission to see any of the reports that were held on these students and in the end judged her attempt at change to be only partially successful. In order to understand this, we need to sketch in some more detail of what she did, and why.

The intervention

Joan had a list of eleven things that she wanted to do to improve her teaching of these students. They ranged from obtaining information from other organisations, through improving the amounts of information that she obtained from in-house procedures like discussions with parents and the screening assessments, to better ways of using this better information within the teaching team for her course. Joan was driven by a deep sense of the professional rightness of this intervention. It would help all of her team to teach better. But her sense of professionalism drove her deeper than this – she felt that she had *a right* to be a party to this information. It made no sense to her that a number of other agencies were deciding on the appropriate post-school progression for these students but doing so without real knowledge of the unique nature of the course (Joan's) that the students were being directed to. As a professional, Joan did not understand why the FE teacher was not thought to be an appropriate party to these discussions, particularly as non-teachers were discussing issues of education.

As with many FE teachers, Joan felt a bit vulnerable about initiating change at this policy level. However, she gained strength to do this from two sources – her moral and professional belief in the rightness of the change, and her involvement in the research which she felt gave her a certain right to ask questions of people who she would not normally speak to, let alone ask them to justify their policy.

Why she did it

Joan seemed to have four different, if overlapping, purposes in wanting to bring about change in this area. In the first place, and most simply, she was interested in having better information that would be likely to help her in communicating with both students and parents. Second, she believed that knowing more about the students would lead to better teaching. Many of the tests that had been used in the college were in her view inadequate compared to the kind of information that could be gleaned from people in schools who had worked with those students in recent years. Third, Joan had something of a more political agenda as well. She championed the idea of sound educational work being overseen by a *team*, especially in the case of students with special educational needs. In Joan's view, an effective team would keep the whole learner to the fore, helping to guard against the fragmentation of the student's programme into a series of inputs dealing with different skills and capacities. But as well as its emphasis on a pedagogic and professional value-position, the idea of the team also appeared to indi-cate Joan's wish to consolidate a secure base for her work that would make it less vulnerable to challenge from senior figures in the college. It also chimed with Joan's perception of the changing composition of the tutor workforce, where staff were increasingly part-time and had a greater diversity of roles, and needed opportunities to build coherence in working together. Finally, and connected with her participation in the TLC project, Joan felt able to ask new and more searching questions about how she and the college were positioned in systems and practices. For example, she wondered why it was that information that could help her and colleagues do a good job had, hitherto, been unavailable. Why was FE not trusted to be a party to this information, not trusted to be useful in the post-school progression discussion? Why was FE only the *outcome* of such discussions?

The outcomes and consequences

Measured against her own list of objectives, the intervention was largely successful. For example, Joan had succeeded in discussing the issue with senior figures in the local Connexions Service, and had gained agreements with the head of a feeder special school. She had also initi-ated regular team meetings involving all of the supporting staff, not just the teachers.

However, meeting a list of initial objectives is only one dimension in a rounded appreciation or evaluation of such activity. Joan herself drew attention to the complexity of the situation and, as we will see later, her feelings that in the end the intervention failed:

> I have come to the conclusion that the constraints of time and the
> amount of control within the role of course organiser, has limited

the ability to make changes across the team although most of the key objectives [of the intervention] have been met one way or another. The most significant changes have come from outside, from the Head of School and new initiatives such as the Core Curriculum. The effects this will have on the way teaching takes place over the whole curriculum will have much more impact than any action a course organiser is able to take.

The area where I can have any control is in the classroom and this is one of the reasons why I have decided to make my action plan for change / intervention only within my teaching for next year. The other reasons are because I have decided to reduce my working hours next year and the Head of School has decided to give the course organiser responsibility to another member of staff.

Rachel's story: 'a better course for the students'

At Whitehills College, one of Rachel's major interventions while associated with the project was to replace a Travel and Tourism AVCE for which she was responsible with a BTEC National Diploma in the same subject area. Though both courses are classed as level 3 and full-time, and have the same entry criteria, the former is deemed equivalent to two A levels (traditional advanced-level academic qualifications), and the latter to three. In a general sense, Rachel attributed the decision to make this shift to her participation in the TLC project, which had heightened her critical awareness and exposed her in new ways to student views of their learning experiences.

There appeared to be two specific drivers for Rachel when deciding to make this shift. The first was her weighing up of the capacities, preferences and learning experiences of the group of students. Though 'smaller' in terms of academic equivalence, the AVCE was in fact a more 'academic' course than the BTEC in terms of the nature of its assessment tasks. The more practical orientation of the BTEC would better suit her students' dispositions, and together with a colleague, she came to the view that it was 'more in touch with the industry'. Second, the BTEC course required students to be timetabled over four days, where the AVCE fitted into three. Rachel reasoned that this pattern of required attendance would be more likely than the earlier one to promote student engagement with and commitment to the course, not least through reducing the amount of time available for part-time work.

The intervention resulted in both change and continuity in the learning culture. Many aspects remained the same, as Rachel used much of the AVCE teaching material for the BTEC where units covered similar ground, and she incorporated into the BTEC a number of additional short courses that she had previously added to the AVCE syllabus (for example, a short course on Air Ticketing). The more visible changes were the removal of exams, the more practical orientation to many of the assignments (with consequent pedagogical changes) and the introduction of regular work placements.

There were several easily measurable outcomes, favourable according to standard FE measurements and to Rachel herself. Student retention was higher with the BTEC group than it had been with the AVCE cohorts and students were achieving pass grades from the beginning of the course, which had not happened with the AVCE. Rachel attributed these outcomes to the more gradual build-up of assignment-writing skills on the BTEC and to two specific aspects of her practice that she had deliberately changed following her experience with AVCE: her active discouragement of two disruptive students to continue with the course and a much stricter policy over assignment deadlines.

Another, and to Rachel unexpected, outcome was her discovery of how challenging she found it to make changes to her preferred practice of leading from the front (especially for practical activities) and to mark practical assignments. She found this much more difficult than she had anticipated, and concluded that her teaching had become more academic than she had previously acknowledged. She had become accustomed to marking the AVCE type of assignment, and found herself initially less confident with marking on the BTEC. The change to BTEC may have been made partly to be more in tune with Rachel's own predisposition for the practical, but it also revealed that other aspects of her professional disposition had been developing simultaneously, namely feeling more confident with an academic approach to learning. She felt both more at home with the more overtly vocational BTEC, and also less confident – initially at least – in developing a different and appropriate pedagogy.

Making sense of interventions in FE learning cultures

When we look at the ways in which tutors intervene in learning cultures, it becomes clear that the overall reason for intervention is the desire to effect positive change in the learning culture. The focus of most interventions is to create a better situation for students. Whereas many of the interventions we observed throughout the project were indeed deliberate attempts to make changes in one or more aspects of the learning culture, not all were of this character. We also found interventions that were focused on mitigating negative change, rather than bringing about positive change. And we came across a very particular kind of intervention – tutors leaving a course, a college or even teaching as a whole – which we termed 'interventions for exit'. We found, in other words, that interventions themselves were much more multifaceted than we had anticipated. We also found that although interventions begin with the tutor, they always operate in a field constituted by actions and interests of many others. This, as we will now discuss in more detail, shows how difficult it actually can be to change the culture.

Interventions for positive change

What can we learn about improvement from Joan's and Rachel's story? First, Joan's intervention had mixed results. The reports on students that Joan had been promised never actually materialised. There was no move to involve the FE teachers in the discussions about post-school progression for individual students. The team approach was made untenable as staff were frequently changed and there was no resourcing for the effective involvement of part-time and supporting staff. Most critically of all, Joan's job profile was changed and she was no longer the course organiser. In one sense, Joan discovered some limits to what it was possible to achieve in a particular set of circumstances. Although Joan never felt she enjoyed the support of the Head of School with her intervention, she almost never blamed the Head or team members for negative developments. She seemed to feel that they must all be under intolerable pressures to have failed to take up her initiative on improving the information on individual students, or to have failed to defend a course as good as the one she led. In the end, and not unconnected to her experience with this attempt to achieve change, Joan took voluntary redundancy and left teaching.

Culturally, the intervention challenged existing power relations within the college, and, arguably, it also challenged the clean slate mantra, which is one of the sacred stories of the sector.[2] But for now, we simply want to draw attention to the fact that there are both successes and failures at different levels within this intervention. Underneath its conventional 'improvement of practice' surface, the intervention was in a sense too challenging in relation to the field, and its immanent failure seems directly linked to Joan's subsequent departure from FE. Thus, her final intervention, like that of another of the participating tutors (see p. 118), was to remove herself from the situation. She decided that she could no longer professionally support the course that was on offer to these students.

Rachel's intervention reminds us of how even quite fundamental change, which at first glance looks easy to monitor in conventional terms, is in fact very difficult to evaluate. At the same time as introducing a new curriculum and qualification and all the associated practices, Rachel also encouraged two disruptive students to leave, and introduced a more strict management of assignment deadlines. But even without these two extra, consciously executed changes in practice, it would still be impossible to disentangle the myriad potential causes for the positive outcomes observed. Furthermore there are different ways of reading what is best for the students. We detected that the shift to BTEC may have reduced the challenges students face and reduced some of their opportunity for expansive learning, at the same time as it ushered in a regime of greater synergy with the vocational field (for example, regular work placements, where the AVCE had none). Greater contact with relevant workplaces could well amount to an improvement if the course had a singular vocational purpose. However, we also know that very few of the students actually went on to work in travel and tourism industries. They were using the programme as a general education and many (though by no means all) arrived at it having missed the level of attainment required for the general academic educational route (A levels). There are wider structural implications here. Rachel may be more or less knowingly engaging in an educational process that keeps less academic students in the system while further confirming that they are indeed less academic. Her innovation could be read as having provided the college with a means to do this more effectively than it was done before. This in turn begs the question of what is in the students' best interests. If customer satisfaction and student recruitment, retention and completion are our only yardsticks then perhaps there is no problem.

As with the idea of improvement, good practice is often portrayed as simple, simply adopted and transferable. Indeed, sometimes educational research has been accused of not offering clear enough descriptions, thereby hampering this essential simplicity. This is a mistake on several levels. Leaving aside the most basic problem (i.e., that the features of good practice in one FE setting might well be the opposite in another), the more detailed analysis of our data can reveal some troubling complexity. Take the example of Celia, the tutor whose intervention was the introduction of texting her students on a GNVQ Business Studies programme. Celia used text messages for a variety of purposes, keeping in touch with the difficulties of her tutees as well as helping her to maintain more accurate attendance records through registering agreed absences. The intervention is attractive – even 'sexy'. It relied on some agility and creativity on the part of the tutor. It also got results, in both official and less official terms. Everyone, it appeared, was a winner. But it is far from straightforward, and leads one to suggest that win-win situations need a hard, hard look. While warmly welcomed and easily communicated, this bit of good practice was not taken up *in any sense* by the college. Celia did not get the promised college mobile phone with which to do her texting and in the following year, the freedom of the students to communicate their absence directly with the tutor was curtailed, reverting to the use of an overloaded telephone line directly to an administrator. This apparently simple way of improving teaching and learning was loaded with challenges between professional teachers and managers over who had the right to decide which absence should be recorded as acceptable. This is not a simple issue of administrative convenience or job demarcation – it decides whether student attendance is positioned as part of the learning relationship between teacher and student, or as part of the policing relationship between managers and government over the financing of FE (see also Gleeson 2005 et al.).

Our overall analysis suggests that the FE culture has become a barren environment when it comes to celebrating tutor creativity of this kind. Good practice might not always be the right kind of good practice for each of the interests at stake: the 'texting' intervention took a college system for audit and removed it from the direct gaze of audit – a sort of 'producer capture'. This may not necessarily mean that the college does not trust teachers, but it might mean that it operates in frameworks that avoid the risks associated with unconventional solutions. Celia's intervention makes us ask 'good practice or improvement for whom?' and 'in whose interests?' and 'by whose reckoning?' In the context of teaching and learning in colleges of Further Education, both 'improvement' and 'good practice' are terms that *imply* consensus or common-sense agreement, but which may *conceal* quite fundamental tensions. If we are serious about change for the better in teaching and learning, then this complexity cannot be ignored or avoided.

Intervention to mitigate negative change

There were other examples of attempts to improve teaching and learning – some of them more modest in scope, others more far-reaching and fundamental in the sense that they were bound up with personal and professional change. But for every example of a tutor deciding to do x to make things better, we have several more where tutors' accounts of what they were doing suggest they were reacting to imposed change in ways that they hoped or intended might mitigate – or even cancel out – its potential effects. This is where sets of professional values and practices come into tension or conflict with new expectations or requirements (from college managers, funding arrangements, qualification bodies, and other stakeholders).

In the Administration and IT (vocational course for KS2) learning site, Julia's intervention consisted of attempts to restore some elements of a learning culture that had been removed (the office facility where students could learn and practice skills) or become eroded (for example, the group increasingly taken by other tutors with less 'pre-16' experience). She was clear that such shifts had led to students getting a raw deal. This intervention, or rather series of linked interventions ending with her handing over to someone else, was clearly informed by Julia's pedagogical values and was also in harmony with her changing role in the college. Once she came to occupy a management position in relation to the area of work, she could do something to restore what had been lost. This may also be understood as a move towards greater synergy, not least between tutor and student dispositions.

Some interventions are more clearly described under this heading of 'reinstatement'. Early in the project, our cultural analysis of sites alerted us to the underground working of Gwen (Work-based NVQ Assessment) (see also Chapter 5). Another way of describing Gwen's list of unofficial working practices (see James and Diment 2003: 414–415) is that they are a series of tutor interventions – deliberate attempts to change the nature and scope of the interaction between learners, workplaces, assessment-defined curricular goals and a range of interests. Yet at the same time they are not particularly *interventionist* because they are so in keeping with what Gwen defined as good professional behaviour, a notion that is deeply rooted in her personal and professional history. What her example highlights so well is the importance of *mediation*. Her actions are forged at the cross-over between her model of appropriate professional behaviour and the requirements of her as made explicit in the NVQ assessment regime. Accordingly, our analysis of the learning culture in this site took us into the tutor's history, but also the history of the big ideas behind competence-based assessment and the policy shifts that gave rise to the current, competitive situation. We concluded that 'improvement' was especially difficult to envisage in this site.

The Engineering in Electronics and Telecommunications learning site provided a further example of tutor mediation. John, the tutor, consistently presented himself as having a sound knowledge of his students' best interests, and standing between his students and a whole series of externally imposed changes, many of them quite fundamental. They included changes in the curriculum specification, the assessment regime, even shifting college timetabling constraints with a major potential impact on students. As we saw in Chapter 5, the offer of a one-year version of the two-year course to a new employer client presented the tutor with another opportunity for a fairly major intervention. Unlike some intervening events, which appeared to the tutor to defy reason or comprehension, this one was seen by him as justified because it could help the survival of the programmes (which were collectively suffering a decline in student numbers). But while the intervening events varied, there was a consistency in the tutor's response which appeared to predate his involvement in TLC. He presented his task as always to make the best of the new situation, to minimise or limit the 'damage' to students. When explaining his educational justifications for the need to intervene, he called on both common-sense notions and more professional ideas (for example, student-centredness, unconditional support), often pointing to his teaching qualifications or his former work in a more 'dynamic' segment of FE. Mediation as damage limitation is a useful way of characterising this tutor's interventions, but we should beware of jumping to the conclusion that he really does know best – that he is somehow usually right and his managers usually wrong. In any case, it is not simply a matter of him reacting against the demands of his managers or an awarding body: John complained just as bitterly about some of his colleagues and their lax approach to record-keeping, and about other aspects of their 'dinosaur' culture in his subject area. He recognised that even his best efforts would have small impact overall, but it was not disappointment in the size of his impact but tiredness, illness or retirement that would eventually stop him from working hard to mitigate the impact of external changes on his students.

Intervention for exit

Arguably, a tutor's most radical intervention is to remove themselves from their work. We were surprised by the high proportion of people leaving FE, both among our immediate participants and among other people known to us in the colleges. But setting this aside, it is possible to distinguish between different degrees of exit.

Florence, the tutor in AS French, made a complete exit. Her voluntary redundancy in 2003 not only came at a time of college financial crisis, but also represented the culmination of a longer process. Key events in this were the reduction of hours for teaching and the clash this made with Florence's approach to teaching and indeed her values about the sort of job that was worth doing. Florence had also moved from being highly regarded by college managers, to a position of marginality, in an age in which stricter audit regimes operated. In a sense, her social capital (her good results, some of which could be seen as against the odds, her status as a 'good teacher' etc.) gave her a 'position' in earlier times, but given a series of structural changes since Incorporation,[3] where different capital differentiates, her position in the field became more ambiguous. It became more 'casual' – exactly the term used for her new, temporary, dispensable relationship to the college. Florence made the personal choice to stop trying to do what cannot be done, and to refuse to engage in imposed practices she considered professionally, morally and polit-ically unacceptable. Her decisions also reflected a wider series of shifts (MFL is itself marginalised in the wider system). In this situation, her only options were either denial of her professional habitus, or her self-removal from the field, that is to cease to be a player.

A slightly different, partial notion of intervention for exit appeared in the English for Speakers of Other Languages site. Here, and in the time frame of the TLC project (and indeed partly attributable to it), the tutor Ruth increasingly discovered and pursued new forms of profes-sional sustenance that were located just outside and beyond her college role. She became confident that as a professional she could assert her strong belief that high quality teaching is evidenced by life-change as well as exam results, and her increasing participation in *Reflect ESOL* provided a new focus.[4] We might say she had made manifest the latent political nature of her work (particularly with asylum seekers). What was so interesting about this was that Ruth's sense of self and her professional identity were palpably stronger, despite (1) serious trouble in her part of the college, where the net effect of faculty mergers and geographical relocation of her ESOL work had been to remove it from

its former relatively 'rich' location and to associate it with a serious
funding deficit, and (2) the fact that the site was in one sense highly
directed, because it responded directly to changing government policy
on groups like refugees and asylum seekers, including recent fundamental changes in eligibility rules. Ruth's professional habitus was confirmed
and nurtured by her engagement with new groups and activities that
combine professional and political interests. Significantly, these were
outside the ambit of the college (though she had plans to bring them
in!). Our analysis suggests that this new external context was key to
her sense of self, and therefore to her mediation of the learning culture,
and that it offered her some degree of insulation from the high vulnerability of the provision that formed the core of her teaching.[5]

Towards a different understanding of improvement

The data and analysis we have presented in this chapter raise
uncomfortable questions about the technical notion of change and
improvement that we introduced at the beginning of this chapter. This
idea, like the related idea of evidence-based practice, is simplistic and
therefore unrealistic. It could be termed a technocratic view, because
it assumes that there is general agreement on the *goals* or *ends* of
the educational process, so that it is just a question of finding the most
effective *means* to arrive at those goals or to bring about improvement
in the process.

Although it is a problematic concept, the project made use of interventions as one of its vehicles for looking at learning cultures and tutors
in FE colleges. The result demonstrates that even the most carefully
planned change in apparently favourable circumstances has unantic-
ipated consequences, some of which can even be negative. It also shows
that it is a mistake always to see the tutor as holding all the reins: the
power and reach of a learning culture means that tutors do not act
just as they please. But if the technical model of change falls short
of providing us with a practical knowledge for the improvement of
teaching and learning, what do we propose in its place? What might be
more realistic and perhaps useful?

Before answering this question, we need to reiterate one or two key
points in our overall data and analysis. Looking across our learning
sites, there are many fairly obvious differences in subject matter, level,
mode of working and so on. What was less immediately apparent at the
outset, but just as important, were *the different ways in which learning*

is understood or conceived. The fact that learning sites are institutionally adjacent, or share regimes of funding, audit and inspection, does not mean they share many other elements of learning *culture.* The college that contains Entry Level Drama, aimed at students with special educational needs, also houses many level 3 academic qualifications, and while both sorts of provision are measured in terms of recruitment and retention, even a casual look reveals they encompass very different sets of practices and assumptions. In the Drama site, *learning* is mainly a process of *participation,* while in the academic sites it encompasses strong notions of *acquisition,*[6] a fact reflected in the assessment regimes of the different courses and awards. Differences of this magnitude make us question the idea of unitary notions of good practice. Furthermore, considering our data on *what was actually being learnt,* we were struck by the different (but equally important) departures in each case from official accounts. In the Drama site, we have evidence that students were (among other things) learning *dependency,* while in one A level academic site, we noticed some of the students were learning (among other things) that they were incapable of study in that subject, and they lost confidence. In such cases, the ostensible purposes and limits, as presented in officially sanctioned prescriptions and declarations, are only part of the story.

Making sense of such empirical material went hand in hand with our developing theoretical work. From the outset we had made use of theoretical tools borrowed from Pierre Bourdieu to help us develop a cultural understanding of learning and to keep us focused on social practices. Some way into the project we found that our emerging analysis also had a strong affinity with the work of John Dewey (see Biesta and Burbules 2003), especially in helping us to see the way that learning, professional practice and improvement are conceived and can be conceived. One important example of this is that in a Deweyan view, one cannot pretend that learning can be summed up as the dependent variable in a causal relationship to teaching, curriculum, classroom environment and so on (see Biesta 2004c; Vanderstraeten and Biesta 2006). Learning is always a process of meaning making in a continuous process of transaction between the person and the environment. Rather like Bourdieu's insistence that social practices both enact and reproduce the relationship between the individual's dispositions (*habitus*) and the social field, and that the two are mutually constituting, Dewey's focus on the transaction of human actors (and their *habits*) and their environments supports a similar sophistication in how we look at learning. 'Mediation' captures something of this sophistication.

Within the project, our understanding of the different aspects of learning cultures, together with our data on interventions, made us re-examine some prevailing assumptions about teaching, learning and the role of the professional. In arriving at recommendations for improvement (and rather than trying to publish recipes or models of working that would be very unlikely to 'transfer' from one setting to another) we produced our own *Principles of Procedure* (which are set out in Chapter 8). The principles amount to strong, evidence-based recommendations about what might be done by students, tutors, colleges and government to improve teaching and learning in the Further Education sector. In this regard they not only echo Lawrence Stenhouse's approach, but also reflect a Dewey-informed view of the relationship between research and practice:

> Dewey showed that 'evidence' – if such a thing exists – does not provide us with rules for action but only with hypotheses for intelligent problem solving. If, to put it from a slightly different angle, we want an epistemology that is practical enough to understand how knowledge can support practice, we have to concede that the knowledge available through research is not about what works and will work, but about what has worked in the past. The only way to utilize this knowledge is as an *instrument* for undertaking intelligent professional action.
>
> (Biesta 2007: 17)

From intervention to mediation

The difficulties around discussing improvement in teaching and learning shows up the importance of the concepts we use and how they are related to one another. Both the cases set out at the beginning of this chapter were about *interventions*, or deliberate attempts by tutors to change something for the better. However, while the tutors were very active in this, the cases also illustrated a process that is always *at the same time* about the various structures that they operated within and upon. The two sides of the coin are inseparable.

In the project we used the term 'intervention' as a convenient way of signalling a deliberate moment in a process that is otherwise continuous. Our name for the continuous process is *mediation*. The term 'mediation' can help with visualising the relationship between the actions of people and the various structures within which they happen. We do not mean 'mediation' in the way it is used to refer to conflict resolution or in

certain forms of counselling. Nor are we using it in quite the way that
it figures in cultural or media studies, as a term for the process in which
messages are both offered to and responded to by an audience. Our use
is closest to the use of the term in social theory – particularly the work
of Bourdieu, who developed the Marxist concept of mediation (and to
a lesser extent, Anthony Giddens and Margaret Archer) and a little on
its use in socio-cultural psychology.

Mediation is also one of the core concepts in *Activity Theory*, first
developed by the Russian psychologist Lev Vygotsky (1896–1934).
Vygotsky insisted that when we interact with other people or the environment, we do not do so in some sort of 'pure' or 'direct' sense. Such
contacts are mediated by physical and psychological tools, so that when
we act or think, we do so in terms of patterns that are culturally and
materially established and located. Vygotsky was interested in how it
might be possible to understand the mind, or consciousness, by looking
at 'tool mediation' and by making the *activity system* (rather than the
individual) his unit of analysis. At the same time, he was interested
in how activity can be transformational in two senses – for both of the
person and of the situation. Many socio-cultural theorists have further
developed these ideas, and they continue to do so (for example, Wertsch
1998; Vianna and Stetsenko 2006).

Though it has different core concerns, Bourdieu's social theory
encompasses a similar kind of double focus. As he put it in an interview,
while explaining his concept of *habitus*:

> Social reality exists, so to speak, twice, in things and in minds, in
> fields and in habitus, outside and inside agents. And when habitus
> encounters a social world of which it is the product, it finds itself
> 'as a fish in water', it does not feel the weight of the water and it
> takes the world about itself for granted.
>
> (Bourdieu 1989: 43)

As even this short quote shows, Bourdieu's social theory owes much to
his early struggles with two different paradigms in anthropology – one
dealing in structural and universal features of culture, the other dealing
with experiences and meanings held by individuals. His notion of social
practice refers to a form of mediation, because it is always about *both*
the individual's authentic agency *and* the structures (like language, or
social class) that enmesh individual persons and which they constantly
enact. An everyday example might be where a tutor decides to give a
high mark to a student's piece of work: this is clearly a personal and

professional decision, so is clearly 'agentic'. But whether the tutor likes it or not, or knows it or not, their act is at the same time reproducing something more 'structural', such as particular interpretations of criteria, or 'standards'; power relationships; even just 'the way things are and have to be'. In a small way, it might also contribute to a qualification outcome that subsequently impacts on the student's life chances.

As described in Chapter 1, the TLC project was from its inception informed by the thinking of Bourdieu. In particular, we wanted to remain open to the sense in which any aspect of the culture of learning is likely to be joined up to a whole series of other aspects. To put this another way, the actions of both tutors and students should be approached *relationally* if we were to have any chance of understanding them. We argued that most of the time learning is treated in a way that disgorges it from context and treats it as either a technical issue or a psychological issue. This gives it an attractive simplicity, but at too great a cost.

There is in fact a need for a concept like mediation in any attempt to reconcile or move beyond 'the problem of structure and agency'. This is the conflict between the idea that people are either basically driven by culture or, conversely, are completely free agents. In Archer's work (see, for example, Archer 2003), mediation takes place via 'internal conversations', or 'reflexive deliberations', in which people's plans to act are forged in terms of social and cultural circumstances. Their projects or narratives meet various constraints and affordances. In doing all this, of course, people make genuine choices (though not in circum-stances of their own choosing) and they also contribute to shaping the circumstances for everyone else.

Conclusion: changing the culture

In this chapter we have asked how learning cultures can be changed intentionally and what the role of tutors in such processes can be. One conclusion that we wish to draw from our analysis is that while tutors are almost always central to the learning culture, their capacity to effect genuine changes that impact upon the quality of teaching and learning is easily, and commonly, overestimated. Tutors can make a difference and in many of our learning sites we found evidence that tutors do make a difference. What our cultural view of learning makes visible is that tutors and their activities are but one of the constituents of a learning culture and that there are many other factors at play as well, some of them well beyond the control and immediate visibility of the actors in the culture. This not only helps to understand why the power of tutors to change learning cultures is limited, but also, more importantly, helps to understand why interventions for improvement take the different shapes that we found through our research, namely 'positive' interventions for improvement, interventions to mitigate negative change, and interventions for exit. Our research also showed that tutors are differently positioned to bring about improvement. There are, in other words, important differences between the positions that tutors have in learning cultures, which makes some of them more powerful in effecting change than others. We have also seen – and this is important to bear in mind in discussions about improvement as well – that improvement is a highly contested idea in the FE context, which means that part of the struggle over improvement is actually about what counts and is recognised as improvement. All this stands in stark contrast to a 'technical' view of improvement in which, as we described at the beginning of this chapter, it is assumed that improving teaching and learning is a matter of implementing the 'right' means and techniques. Our research shows that improvement is always a matter of changing the culture, and since cultures are complex entities that are partly beyond the control of the main participants – tutors and students – improvement requires not only a better understanding of the complexities of learning cultures. It also requires awareness that improvement always involves judgements both about the means and about the ends of education. After all, what counts as effective 'crucially depends on judgments about what is educationally desirable' (Biesta 2007: 5), and this continually draws attention to who has the power to define how that looks. Empowering teachers to bring about positive change in learning cultures thus requires a broad understanding of their position as professionals. It is to this question that we turn next.

Notes

1   This chapter builds upon substantial contributions from Graham Anderson, Helen Colley, Jennie Davies, Kim Diment, Denis Gleeson, Phil Hodkinson, Wendy Maull, Keith Postlethwaite, Tony Scaife, Michael Tedder and Eunice Wheeler.

2   By 'clean slate mantra' we refer to a widely held view that on many courses, Further Education can best serve its learners by not taking past educational achievements as a reliable source of evidence about the individual's capabilities or potential. This constitutes a refusal to stereotype on the basis of past educational 'failure' and sometimes reflects an insistence that such outcomes tell us more about the institutions and systems than they do about the individuals who are subject to them.

3 'Incorporation' refers to the process in which, following the Further and Higher Education Act 1992, Further Education colleges moved out of the control of the local democratic structures and became free-standing in relation to a central government funding mechanism.

4 *Reflect ESOL* draws on the ideas of Paolo Freire. Perhaps the most central of these is that no educational action is neutral – it is either oppressive or liberatory. *Reflect ESOL* advocates an approach to literacy that refuses narrower, technicist notions of skills and purpose.

5 Further analysis of our data on such cases led us to a new perspective on professionalism and in particular, challenged the idea that it is 'normal' for a person in a profession to move in one direction as they 'become' someone more central in a 'community of practice'. The professional lives of the people in our study were much more dynamic than this, so we realised a need to account for them in more dynamic terms. We suggest that for many, 'unbecoming' is also a helpful notion in trying to explain what is happening (see Chapter 7; see also Colley et al. 2007).

6 For a discussion of these metaphors for learning, see Sfard (1998). Their significance in relation to learning outcomes for a range of educational research projects in the Teaching and Learning Research Programme is addressed in Brown and James (2005). For a view of learning different from both acquisition and participation see Biesta (2004a).

Chapter 7

Professionality in FE learning cultures

Introduction

What constitutes professionalism in FE is an elusive concept. Although professional work in FE has been subjected to a plethora of initiatives in recent years, little is known about its practitioners, their dispositions and how they define their sense of professionalism in the changing context of their work. In Chapter 6, however, we saw how tutors have a direct impact on teaching and learning, there are other changes that tutors make that are more to do with mitigating the effects of changes imposed from elsewhere – outside the particular learning site, or outside the college. We also saw why it is that improvement is far from being a simple matter of finding what works and implementing it. Learning cultures are complex, and always partly beyond the reach of the participants in any particular situation, and improvement always entails judgements about what is educationally desirable. If genuine change for the better involves changing the learning culture, then we need to pay some attention to the scope for practitioners in FE to define what is educationally desirable. We are not implying that their judgements will always be the best ones: rather, that it is important to acknowledge *the ways in which practitioners engage with the other elements of the learning culture.* Accordingly, this chapter gives brief attention to how people become practitioners in FE and the importance of ideas of flexibility. It then looks at professional dispositions and practices, illustrating how challenges to practitioners' judgements are played out, and argues that 'mediation', together with 'field' and 'habitus', are concepts that offer a more subtle grasp of what happens than 'compliance/non-compliance'. We give a brief account of how the TLC project has taken forward its

Authored by David James and Denis Gleeson

analysis of professionality and conclude that, contrary to managerialist tendencies, professionality has to be understood as a fundamental feature of a learning culture, and it is therefore also fundamental to the improvement of teaching and learning in the context of what Foster (2005: 33) refers to as 'the new discourse' of FE.

Getting in: becoming a practitioner in FE

The TLC participating tutors' backgrounds illustrated something of the range of ways in which people become FE practitioners, confirming the widely held perception that many FE practitioners begin their careers in Further Education with no formal training or background in teaching. Many never envisaged professional careers, let alone in teaching, and some slipped into the role through a range of unforeseen and unplanned events. Most had technical skills and qualifications, and many had substantial industrial, commercial or public sector experience directly related to what they were teaching. In many cases, former trade and occupational identities remained important and were called upon in a variety of ways (see Gleeson and Mardle 1980), though we also saw examples of the new 'learning professional', Guile and Lucas's term for those in a new set of roles whose work operates across academic and vocational divisions (Guile and Lucas 1999). The diversity in the composition of the group of tutors in many FE colleges is itself an important and distinctive feature of the learning culture that often goes unrecognised outside the sector.

Rachel, who had a successful career in the travel industry, spoke of 'sliding' into FE following a divorce and a wish for a fresh start. Once teaching, she gained both the City and Guilds 730 and the Certificate in Education (FE) qualifications through part-time study. Even so, she talks of the decision as a pragmatic one: 'It's not a vocation for me and in fact if I didn't have the children I don't think I'd be here today'. For Paul, who taught photography, the decision to teach in FE was both vocational and pragmatic at the same time. First of all he did a small amount of evening class teaching alongside his work as a professional photographer, and found it enjoyable and rewarding. Within a few years he decided to teach full time, and to do what he called 'photography for me' alongside it. His income from teaching meant that it did not matter very much whether or not he sold the photographic work he was producing and exhibiting. John started teaching when the college needed urgent cover for a particular area of work in which he was skilled and knowledgeable. At the same time, his work in electrical

appliance repair had begun to decline, and he consciously fished for
more teaching:

> I got to know a few people . . . and so eventually I sort of spent
> time sitting on the boss's doorstep, 'til he knew me well enough
> and I got a yearly contract, and then a full-time contract.

Many new FE practitioners experience what we might term the 'long
interview', where the individual starts with a few part-time hours, and,
having established a link with a college, is offered more work or a full-
time post after a period of months or years. Gwen recalls making a
difficult decision to leave a secure, full-time office job in order to take
up an insecure, part-time one in FE teaching:

> [I thought] shall I take a chance, because you can't get a job at any
> of the colleges, well certainly not in our faculty, you can't just get
> a full-time job off the streets. You have to be tried and tested. So I
> gave up my [full-time, secure] job and went part-time.

Gwen then worked part-time for two years, at three different colleges,
before being offered the full-time post that she had wanted all along.

These recruitment processes have been an established part of FE
practice for a long time, and reflect the sector's wide range of purposes
(Foster 2005), its entrepreneurial nature and its multifaceted links
with a wide range of workplaces and interests. Compared to schools,
colleges live with a high degree of uncertainty about demand for their
services from one year to the next (and sometimes over a much shorter
timescale) as they respond to market fluctuations and shifts in policy
of the sort discussed in Chapter 3. In recognising these features of the
context, it is no surprise that the recruitment of staff who teach is a
process often characterised by informality and uncertainty, in which
flexibility is a key asset. There are clear benefits for colleges, and sometimes to individual practitioners too. Yet these come at a high price.
The widespread use of fractional and temporary contracts has laid
down distinctions between core and peripheral staff. Together with the
proliferation of job titles in recent years and the low morale engendered
by a lack of parity of esteem and reward with other parts of the education system, this contributes to the casualisation of the FE workforce
(Mackney 2004; Foster 2005). In one of our learning sites, the fact that
so many of the staff were on small part-time contracts meant that Joan,
the coordinator of the area of work, could not bring staff together to

function effectively as a team to achieve improvements, in a pattern we know was repeated elsewhere (see Chapter 6). Moves to a fully qualified workforce (see DfES 2006) may increasingly constrain such flexibility in the next few years, as the investment that would-be teachers and colleges must make will increase.

The flexibility we mentioned remains a facet of work for many – perhaps most –practitioners if they become more established in colleges. While some welcome the chance to work in new fields, it is quite common to find people working outside their comfort zone in colleges, at least for some of the week, teaching a unit or module in an area they feel is beyond their field of expertise but simultaneously feeling they cannot or should not refuse to do so. John's example of this was teaching a unit on microprocessors when his own field was electrical engineering. John described how there was 'no one else to do it'. He found it 'a painful experience really because [I was] so isolated, and [I was] never quite sure whether [I was] doing it right or not'. Paul provides another example, whereby in a context of falling student numbers and job vulnerability, he agreed to take on a leadership role, not in the area of photography, but for a whole range of media courses. As he put it, 'I ended up running media courses because someone had to, and I was one of the more flexible folk around. I ended up flexing myself out of what I like doing best'. Paul described a difficult series of negotiations in which he had to be very assertive in order to 'get back' to being a teacher and leader in the area of photography. Flexibility is also visible over the course of a professional biography. George, a business studies tutor, spoke in several interviews about his loss of professional identity and status accompanying a move from being an accredited subject specialist with experience as an economist, to becoming a teacher of courses aimed at students, in what he described as a 'welfare' function. This perceived shift from teaching to welfare, which arose in a number of interviews and meetings with him, reflects an important shift in the FE sector and the students it serves. For George himself it represents a 'wake of status' that became the defining issue of his professional identity.

Being in FE: professional dispositions and practices

If variety, informality, uncertainty and flexibility are regular features of the recruitment process and work situation of some FE practitioners, what ideas about *professionality* are present in colleges, and how important is this concept in the way that FE practitioners see their work? We found a great deal of complaint and disillusionment around some of the key attributes associated with professional status – with pay, regimes of audit and inspection, a perceived decline in resources, lack of recognition of expertise, reduced autonomy through performance management and so forth. Yet these complaints did not come from a shared political position. They arose from strong commitments to teaching, to fostering student learning and development, to attending to learners' needs, and to self-development or learning as a professional. Time and again, our data gave us examples of tutor frustration because regimes of funding, management and audit/inspection prevented or made more difficult the exercise of judgement based on experience.

There are many theories and models that seek to define and understand what it is to be a professional. Traditionally, social science has approached questions about this in one of two ways. First, a *functionalist/consensus* view characterises professions in terms of the attributes they might share as occupations and the functions they may serve in society. In this view the distinctive attributes of a profession may include a set of skills based on a body of theoretical knowledge, a clear route to qualification for practitioners, a code of conduct, an ethic of altruism and relatively high rewards. A second approach, which we might term an *ideological/conflict* view, sees professionalism as a strategy for establishing occupational dominance and for gaining a monopoly position, and examines the extent to which professionals' declared altruism is a mask for self-interest. These perspectives, or elements of them, continue to be visible in debates, but they are of limited utility here because they are really attempts to understand why professions exist, rather than offering ways of understanding, in a detailed sense, the nature of professional knowledge and action. More recent analyses have moved closer to this, particularly in education, arguing that teachers are subject to intensification of work (Apple and Jungck 1991); to de-professionalisation (Lawn and Ozga 1988), and to deskilling or to a loss of control over the learning environment (Avis et al. 2002; see also Campbell and Neill 1994; Ashcroft and James 1999). Most recently of all, theorists have sought to understand how professionality engages and interacts with the audit culture, performativity and managerialism and inequalities (Biesta 2004b; Ball 2005; Leathwood 2005), and we return to this concern in the remainder of this chapter.

The participating tutors in the TLC project did see themselves as professionals, and they recognised and valued both the obligations and responsibilities that came with this identity. Whether or not it was currently felt, a sense of autonomy was valued highly – not for its own sake, but because of the necessity for continual adaptation to different learners and circumstances, the opportunity to deal with the unexpected and the serendipitous in student learning, and for solving problems. Many tutors also valued the opportunities they had for their own professional learning and action, an idea closely linked to autonomy. We saw one example of this in Chapter 5, where Ruth cited 'high quality learning' that did not focus on certification, or the specifics of skills attained, but on both the distance travelled by learners and the practical outcomes for their lives. She noted how reflecting on these instances had both fostered and revealed her own learning. Another example would be Florence, who described in her diary both her puzzlement and her joy about how well some of her teaching was going:

> So just a few words about the recent success of the classes. I haven't quite worked out the recipe. They approached the last topic a bit more independently, partly because I finally got round to setting it up that way, partly because I felt more comfortable with the idea that the group work would not be in French so long at it *produced* some French. . . . They all took a mini topic from the main one of health and pursued that through their own reading/tapes/internet or simply through the textbook. Then, after a couple of sessions where group work sharing of information got shoved off the end of the lesson plan . . . I had a rather half-hearted go at getting the students to, first, speak with classmates who'd done the same topic (such things as eating disorders, smoking, sport, drugs etc.) and then asked them to speak with at least two people who had done a different topic. This was the bit that amazed me. I went out of the room for a time, thinking about what I would do next if it wasn't going well. When I came in again, they were all speaking to each other in French (after a fashion) and they were thoroughly engaged in the activity.

This diary entry came from a tutor who, not long after writing it, had left FE in the wake of reductions in the contact hours allowed for the course which in her judgement made it impossible to teach properly (see textbox in Chapter 4; see also Colley et al. 2007). The TLC project itself generated a space for participating tutors like Ruth and Florence *to reflect* upon their position and their practice and to some extent, to research their pedagogic thinking. However, it is important not to confuse either what tutors value or the celebrated moments with what tends to pertain the rest of the time, and our cultural approach was, above all, an attempt to find out what was normally the case, or what goes without saying in the normal practices of a learning site.

Overall, what was normally the case added up to a more depressing picture. Many tutors felt bound to an externally monitored cycle of recruitment, retention and certification linked to college funding, remuneration and quality measurement (see Bloomer 1998). Rachel, for example, expressed the view that despite claims to the contrary, external inspection appeared more focused on teacher performance than on student learning. In her diary she described a lesson that had been observed by a senior colleague in preparation for a forthcoming Ofsted inspection:

> a lesson in which I did absolutely no teaching but the outcomes were great in learning terms. . . . It was amusing to be told that as no teaching had taken place, she [the senior colleague] could not give me adequate feedback on the 'lesson' as a whole, although she could not fault the activities, the students' commitment and dedication to the task, and the outcome was clearly that a high degree of learning had taken place. This latter point was endorsed by the students who said that they had enjoyed the activity and felt that they had learned a lot and it was helpful towards being able to complete a written assignment.

Rachel is questioning the idea that 'teaching' always means observable teacher talk or the directing of students 'from the front' in real time, which, rightly or wrongly, a senior colleague had decided would need demonstrating to ensure success in a forthcoming inspection. In this example, a strong and specific notion of pedagogy is enshrined in the measurement of practice, but it is a notion that Rachel finds unrealistic, unhelpful and contrary to evidence. The instance has parallels with the experience of Paul and his colleagues, who (as we saw in Chapter 5) found themselves undoing a major curricular and pedagogic initiative because it did not fit with the expectations of audit. There are further similarities with the case of Gwen (see Chapter 5), where the 'assessment only' NVQ provision depended upon her facilitation of 'underground learning' but at the same time made her detailed support for learners invisible. Gwen was in no position to complain about something she should not have been doing at all in the official eyes of the college.

But what can we say about how practitioners handle such episodes, and what it means to be a professional in such circumstances? Rachel wrote that the contradiction in inspection was 'amusing', but this point was expressed in the relative safety of a TLC project diary entry, and was written to be shared with what she expected would be a sympathetic audience. What is more important is that in her day-to-day work, she was *not in a position* to challenge the orthodoxy that the episode represented. Put another way, the narrow pedagogic perspective driven by the anticipation of inspection was to remain uninformed by Rachel's professional experience. At first glance the reactions of Rachel, Paul and Gwen may appear as simple 'compliance', albeit reluctant. With more detailed analysis, however, we think it is a mistake to see these and other tutors in the project as simply 'complying' with instructions. Wallace and Hoyle (2005) suggest that research into the impact of educational reforms on professional practices shows a high incidence of unintended consequences, ambiguity and wasted effort. In the light of this, they advocate an 'ironic' perspective for understanding the situation of the managed professional. This in turn leads them to argue for *temperate* policy, which by being less totalising and more incremental, has a much greater probability of success. However, they acknowledge that this would only be possible if the makers of policy could place a higher trust in professionals than is apparent in contemporary reforms.

Wallace and Hoyle (2005) also argue that while individual staff do of course respond differently, their responses can be categorised into compliance, non-compliance and mediation. Compliance can be willing or reluctant, and non-compliance can run from mere retreat into current practices through to outright resistance. Wallace and Hoyle (2005) then argue that the concept of *mediation* is a more useful characterisation of many responses because it does not oversimplify and it recognises the ambiguity and irony of the situation while also giving due regard to the sincerity of the endeavour among many professionals as they try to work round externally imposed requirements:

> [Mediating professionals] express what we regard as *principled infidelity*. Infidelity follows from not fully adhering to policy-makers' expectations, and principled follows from attempting to sustain their professional values instead of embracing the alternative values under-girding reforms.
>
> (Wallace and Hoyle 2005: 12)

This is close to the concept of mediation we outline towards the end of Chapter 6. There are also strong parallels here with the concept of *strategic compliance* (Gleeson and Shain 1999). Rather like the actions of people in a nation-state that is occupied by a foreign power, these tutors are playing along with (and sometimes excelling in the terms of) the oppressor's game, while at the same time, keeping alive a separate idea of who they are and where their heart is. While apparently conforming, all found ways to provide their learners with things that *they* valued and knew were valuable. This insight gives us a glimpse of the complexity of cultural change and is a reminder of the major problem with managerialism. Managerialism (which should not be confused with either management or leadership) 'is underpinned by an ideology which assumes that all aspects of organisational life can and should be controlled. In other words, that ambiguity can and should be radically reduced or eliminated' (Wallace and Hoyle 2005: 9). Wallace and Hoyle also argue that, by virtue of having backed a managerialist means to realising reform after reform, 'policy-makers have apparently failed to comprehend the nature of professional practice' (2005: 10). There are gender issues here too. As Hey and Bradford (2004: 693) note, audit and managerialism 'are practices written on bodies' and therefore inextricably linked to gender differences. They demand self-work from tutors to negotiate conflicting images of professional authenticity and autonomy (which themselves are often masculinised) and middle-class, feminised ideas of the caring professional as the 'good mother' (Shain 2000; Reay 2001; Walkerdine 2003).

There is a strong affinity between a belief in managerialism and a continuing tendency to see professionalism as old-fashioned, as self-serving and as incapable of a flexible response to client need – and therefore as the wrong place to look for the generation of improvement. Although it has in the past had clearest political expression from socialists (perhaps most famously in George Bernard Shaw's 1906 play *The Doctor's Dilemma*), the more recent promotion of this view came from the Thatcher conservative government and was part of what Gewirtz (2002) refers to as the post-welfarist education policy complex and an associated manufacture of a new common sense. Gewirtz (2002) quotes Fergusson (1998):

> Teachers were denigrated as self-interested and unaccountable. And while self-interest is normalized as part of the discourse of market relations, and elsewhere is celebrated as the engine of progress, it is seen in this instance as invalidating teachers' claims

to professionalism. Other routes to breaking bureau professional power entailed the public questioning of the competency of teachers, allegations of the failure of the comprehensive system, the down-skilling of teachers' professional knowledge through the exclusion of theory in favour of more instrumental forms of initial training and in-service staff development.

(Fergusson 1998: 230)

This, arguably, concerted attack on an established concept of professionalism was also bound up with a more widespread rising distrust of bureaucracy, a reassertion of the rights of the individual as customer, and the rise of the market and managerialism in the public sector. At the time of writing, a similar theme finds expression in political thinking about the improvement of public services. One senior government figure has described how such improvement can only come out of a pincer-like movement in which the recent growth in top-down regulation through targets and standards is augmented by a new encouragement to bottom-up mechanisms for greater consumer or user 'voice'. In the middle of these two movements is an idea of the professional as simply someone who does a thorough job exactly in line with some sort of specification such as a service agreement (see Miliband 2006).

However, our analysis of learning cultures shows that, crudely speaking, a conscious sense of professionalism is not eradicated by increasing prescription. Furthermore, rather than representing an obstacle to improvement, professionality is actually fundamental to it, because it is a crucial existing aspect of the learning culture, a facet of the reality of teaching and learning that it is unrealistic to ignore. We think it is most helpful to conceive the professional *habitus* of tutors as a set of 'durable, transposable dispositions' (Bourdieu 1990: 53) that were often generated in different, prior circumstances. As embodied facets of those different, prior circumstances or fields, there will be limits to the synergy between these dispositions and the *field* that the tutors now find themselves within. In the case of Gwen, the relevant change in the field is the progressive segregation of learning and assessment, which might be termed the hallmark of the curriculum changes brought in by National Vocational Qualifications. In turn, this meant that a key part of her *professional capital*, which was pedagogical knowledge, was no longer 'rated' so highly in the *field* (see James and Diment 2003). By contrast, newly employed practitioners on 'assessment only' contracts had a more constrained, contractual relationship with the learners, and appeared to operate without the dissonance experienced by

Gwen (though she suggested their success rates were not as high as her own).

It is important to note that an understanding of professionality as the relationship between habitus and field does not rely on the sort of normative grounds of everyday accounts. For example, in conventional terms, professionals who are critical of change can find themselves accused of 'golden ageism' (the idea that things were always better in the past), or of harbouring a self-interested lack of flexibility or resistance to change. Both these accusations are normative, in that they are pejorative. By contrast, we are arguing here that an established professional identity can be compromised simply by being located in a new field (much as a given amount of money can be worth little or nothing if taken into a country with a different currency). After this it is a separate empirical question as to whether things were better in the past or whether the individuals involved are reacting conservatively.

Professionality in a learning culture

There can be little doubt that in fields like education and healthcare, the life of the professional, and what it means to be a professional, has become more complex and contradictory in recent decades. Gleeson et al. (2005) draw on TLC project data to examine this complexity in relation to FE practitioners as a 'case in point', arguing that they work in one of the most 'market tested' sectors of public provision that amounts to an internationally significant 'prototype' of market-driven reforms that have 'radically altered democratic accountability in favour of government, business and corporate interests' (Gleeson et al. 2005: 447). A key aspect of their analysis questions the idea that there is a 'community of professional practice' in FE and argues that one needs to be built. However, building professional capacity in FE also requires new *theories* of professionalism that can guide pedagogy and practice since the pragmatism of FE practice – the 'culture of the now' – is incapable of achieving such change alone.[1]

Gleeson et al. 2005 state that FE professionals are usually seen *either* as subject to external reform *or* as active agents who can and do construct identity and meaning within their work (echoing Bathmaker's (2001) 'dupes or devils' distinction). However, they argue, professional knowledge is generated as the tensions are experienced 'between external criteria of performance and those "ecologies of practice" (Stronach et al. 2002) that frame identity and reality making among FE professionals' (Gleeson et al. 2005: 455–456). This argument is supported by data from the TLC project, and it demonstrates the need for subtlety in any attempt to understand the role of professionality in contemporary practices. There are strong similarities with Wallace and Hoyle's argument, mentioned previously, for a concept of *mediation* that helps us see beyond the cruder notions of compliance and non-compliance. However, where Wallace and Hoyle (2005) see grounds for optimism if reforming policies can be made more 'temperate' (so that such policies acknowledge the essential ambiguity of the worlds of practice they seek to change), Gleeson et al. (2005) offer a more pessimistic prognosis. For them, the isolated and individualised 're-storying' of FE practitioners cannot add up to the generation of stronger shared notions of professionalism. Though constantly faced with decisions about compliance or contestation and with opportunities to be creative (see Stronach et al. 2002; Ranson 2003), practitioners are located in a fragmented FE sector with little sense of history (the 'culture of the now' mentioned above). Gaining a stronger sense of professionality would require a more fundamental shift in the relationships that produce it, perhaps through professionals enjoying higher levels of trust but also being more answerable to civil society, which, it could be argued, is the source of the authority implied by the term 'professional'. Perhaps a stronger sense of professionality could come from 'the restoration of wider forms of democratic governance and accountability . . . which transcend market narratives and consumerist concerns' (Gleeson et al. 2005: 456). Thus, a cultural understanding of learning implies that professionalism does not simply occur *in* a social context but operates *as* a social practice and constitutes a highly contested process. This, in turn, draws attention to the significance of power relations in FE, in wider society and in individual learning sites.

The idea of a 'community of practice' of professionals is challenged in another way within the TLC project. One common-sense view of professional work is that, on the whole, people gain experience over time and become more established, becoming located, as it were, more 'centrally'. The direction of movement implied here seems to fit with a popular contemporary theory of situated learning, the most well-known expression of which is that of Lave and Wenger (1991). Put simply, this social theory of learning does not dwell on the cognitive or mental processes that may be involved in learning, but on social arrangements and mechanisms. Novices enter a community of practice and engage at first in 'legitimate peripheral participation'. Over time, they move towards expertise and full membership and full participation. The theory is about both the social relations of learning *and* the conditions for the existence of any form of professional knowledge, and hence the existence of knowledgeable practitioners themselves (see Fuller et al. 2005).

Hodkinson and Hodkinson (2004) note that the communities of practice idea has become 'iconic' in recent years. However, along with some other established academic and policy constructs, the periphery-to-centre movement at the core of situated learning did not turn out to be a helpful framework when we looked across the professional trajectories of the FE tutors who participated in the TLC project. As Colley et al. (2007), writing just after the end of the fieldwork, put it:

> Of the 24 tutors who participated in the project, only about a third remain committed to teaching in the sector.[2] Three left FE to move into sixth form provision, two have become full-time managers and are no longer teaching, five have either quit their jobs or been made redundant, and five give accounts of themselves as marginalized, and are making serious efforts to leave FE (some have already reduced their hours to part-time).
>
> (Colley et al. 2007: 174)

We do not claim that the twenty-four tutors were a classically representative sample of all the staff who teach in FE colleges in England. However, as noted in Chapter 1, the learning sites and participating tutors were chosen carefully, in a process of balancing the wishes of college managements with a need for purposive choices of case (Flyvbjerg 2006) that would reflect the diversity of provision in the sector. The learning sites suggested for inclusion by colleges were not those they felt were particularly problematic, weak or vulnerable. Indeed, having worked for a time with the colleges, we learnt that many of the learning sites offered to the project had internal reputations for being relatively successful. This makes the figures quoted by Colley et al. (2007) all the more poignant and somewhat at odds with the bland assertions of a passionate, committed and professional workforce in the Foster Report (2005: para 249).

Conclusion

The Review of Further Education carried out by Sir Andrew Foster (2005) had the following to say about the people who work in Further Education:

Almost a quarter of a million people are currently employed in FE colleges across England. They are the most vital resource that FE colleges have. In the course of the review it was clear that focused, committed and professional lecturers, support staff and leaders have transformed individual lives and make a real difference to local businesses.

(Foster 2005: 73)

The same report went on to note a series of existing measures 'to improve the quality and professional standing of the workforce and its leadership'. These include reforms to teaching and learning overseen by the DfES Standards Unit, improvements to teacher training, the setting up of Lifelong Learning UK to develop standards for the sector (see LLUK 2006) and the 'embryonic' Institute for Learning, a new professional body (see IfL 2006). It recommended that in addition to these moves, 'a new national workforce development strategy be produced, led by the DfES, founded on a fresh analysis of workforce needs' (Foster 2005: 74). The White Paper, appearing in March 2006 and drawing heavily on Foster's report, contained a whole chapter on 'A national strategy for teaching and learning in Further Education' in which plans were set out to lead a quality improvement strategy including new forms of support for teaching staff, materials, and subject coaches. The Strategy would also 'support increasing personalisation', and contain a new drive to develop the workforce, including a requirement for Continuing Professional Development (DfES 2006).

There is a danger – and many would put it stronger, as a probability – that across this continuing raft of reforms, only the narrowest notions of professionalism are allowed to prevail. The analyses of both Gleeson et al. and Colley et al. draw on TLC project data to show that understanding professionality in Further Education colleges requires a subtle approach that takes cognisance of the other major influences on the learning culture. A managerialist perspective allows only a *reduced* or *restricted* concept of professionality, such as might be heard in connection with any service carried out to a high standard ('we offer fully professional carpet cleaning', for example). The data and analysis of the TLC project illustrate how important an *expanded* concept of professionality remains, even in the face of repeated and pervasive challenges to the autonomy and scope for self-determination of the practitioners. If we are serious about change-for-the-better in teaching and learning, it is indefensible to ignore the ways that professionality currently figures in practice.

Notes

1   The 'culture of the now' concept was initially used in an internal project paper by Wahlberg; see also Scaife (2004).
2   This figure of twenty-four tutors includes the original sixteen participating tutors (one for each learning site); three replacement tutors when sites changed or ceased operation; the four 'FE-based research fellows', i.e., FE practitioners seconded to the project for four-tenths of their posts; one replacement for one of these research fellows.

Part III

What are the overall implications?

Chapter 8

Transforming learning cultures in Further Education

Introduction

In this book we have tried to give an answer to the question of how teaching and learning in Further Education might be improved. Our answer, as we already stated in Chapter 1, is deceptively simply: *Change the culture!* But as we have shown in several chapters, transforming a learning culture is more easily said than done. This is first of all because learning cultures are complex and multifaceted entities. Although one might be able to influence some of the factors that shape a learning culture, other factors may be much more difficult or even impossible to change. Changing the culture is also difficult because learning cultures are made by people. Learning cultures, as we have argued, are not the environments in which people learn but the social practices through which they learn, which means that they exist through the actions, dispositions and interpretations of the participants. This does not mean that the participants in a particular learning culture are completely free to construct the learning culture in any way they want. Many of the examples in this book show the constraints under which tutors, students and college managers have to operate. Such constraints are partly cultural, partly structural, and partly ideological, in that they have to do with prevailing ideas about the point and purpose of Further Education and about good teaching and worthwhile learning. Improving learning cultures in FE therefore not only entails the transformation of the immediate practices of teaching and learning themselves, but also draws attention to the wider factors that constitute those cultures and

Authored by Gert Biesta, David James, Phil Hodkinson, Denis Gleeson and Keith Postlethwaite practices. Finally, transforming learning cultures is not easy because learning cultures are not static but are themselves always in trans-formation.

Although it is not easy to change a learning culture, the overall conclusion of our research is that because learning cultures are partly constructed by people, there is scope for some significant change through which improvements can be brought about. In this final chapter we focus on the ways in which learning cultures might be transformed and on how, through such transformations, learning might be improved. We do this in four steps. We begin with a brief description of four char-acteristics of learning cultures in Further Education that, despite the many differences, were relatively common across most sites in our research. We then present six research-supported broader principles for improving learning in Further Education. Next we discuss four possible 'drivers' for improvement, that is, four constituents of learning cultures which in our view and based on the findings of our research, are crucial for the transformation of learning cultures and the improvement of learning. Taken together, these three sections summarise our main rec-ommendations for the improvement of learning in Further Education. Although we do not believe that research can provide recipes for practice (see also Biesta 2007), we have made an attempt to summarise our main recommendations also in a more concrete way. We have done this in the *Principles of Procedure for Improving Learning in FE*, which is the final section of this chapter. The *Principles of Procedure* focus on the four main drivers for improvement and indicate under each driver what the main players in Further Education – government and national bodies, college management, tutors, and students – should focus on if they are serious about the improvement of learning.

The learning culture of FE

In our research we have looked in detail at the nature of learning cultures in Further Education. We found much variety. Each learning site had a learning culture that was significantly different from others, and within sites we also found difference and change over time, for example, to name but one factor, as the result of the arrival of a new cohort of students. The practices of teaching and learning and the ideas about what counts as 'good' learning and 'good' teaching differed from site to site, as did the dispositions and intentions of students and tutors. Learning cultures in the different sites had differences in practice as well as differences in values. As a result, interventions that worked in one site might not be appropriate in another. Despite the variety that we encountered in our research, we also found commonalities across the learning cultures in FE. They suggest something about the more general learning culture of the sector. It is important for the different parties in the sector to be aware of these more general characteristics if they want to change particular learning cultures for the better.

The central significance of the tutor in learning

Despite the fact that the role and position of tutors has significantly changed over the past decades, and despite the fact that much teaching in Further Education is far less teacher led than it has been in the past, our research confirmed the central significance of the tutor in a wide range of different forms and practices of learning. However, there was considerable variation in tutor position. Some tutors were more independent than others and had more room for manoeuvre. Some were teaching in courses that they had started themselves; others had to deliver courses of which they actually disapproved.

Status and qualification hierarchies

The Further Education sector (excluding sixth form colleges) has always dealt with students, young and old, looking for a second chance in education. Often these are people for whom schooling has been problematic. These are often working-class students and/or students from minority backgrounds. Further Education has developed a welcoming ethos and a set of practices to work with such students. However, this has contributed to its relatively low status compared with schools and Higher Education, and this status permits forms of funding and managerialism that are more extreme than in other education sectors. The status issue impacts on different courses and sites in different ways, often risking detriment for those on lower-status routes within the Further Education portfolio. This is more than the distinction between academic and vocational. There are significant hierarchies within and between vocational qualifications which affect recruitment, progression and student and tutor identity.

Inadequate funding and a rigid audit regime

Learning in Further Education is pressured and destabilised by a combination of inadequate and unstable funding and a rigid audit regime, focused on retention, achievement and inspection standards. This leads to a situation in which tutors spend much of their time striving to protect the existing learning culture from external damage – such as dramatic reductions in class contact time, imposed register systems that do not fit with patterns of attendance and learning, and tensions between inclusion and high achievement rates. Dealing with this entails extensive underground working, with many tutors routinely engaged in working well beyond their job descriptions, simply to keep classes afloat. Our evidence suggests that these pressures increased during the period of the research, with increasingly detrimental effects. Rather than improving learning, such managerial approaches threatened its quality, and tutors were running out of the energy and morale needed to resist them.

External 'agenda setting'

Pressures to improve teaching and learning in Further Education are primarily externally driven and generally by concerns other than the nature of teaching and learning. Since the 1950s, as we have shown in Chapter 3, there have been repeated calls for the improvement of teaching and learning in Further Education to solve perceived social and moral problems among youth; the inadequacy of vocational education and training for employers; insufficient skill levels to ensure the nation's global competitiveness; and the need for a cost-effective Further Education service. Beneath these different calls for improvement, lies a basic problem: the demand that the sector provides effective responses to some of the country's major social, employment and economic needs, whilst maximising cost effectiveness.

Improving learning: six research-supported principles

Significant changes to the management and funding of FE are vital if improvements are to be made. The sector requires stable and adequate funding, and a form of accountability that avoids the pernicious effects of the audit culture of low-trust accountability. Because of this, and because of the variability and complexity within and between FE learning cultures, it is necessary to develop ways to manage and monitor improvements that do not require either universal approaches or over-reliance on measured outputs, which is precisely what we have tried to articulate in the *Principles of Procedure* (see pp. 149–159). Underpinning these lie our six research-supported broader principles about improving learning in FE:

1   Improving learning entails more than increasing its effectiveness. It is important to supplement judgements about learning effectiveness with judgements about the value of learning, and to make issues of effectiveness subordinate to issues of value.
2   There are many different positive learning processes and outcomes, beyond the achievement of a qualification. Different groups and different individuals may appropriately value different things, and operate legitimately with different conceptions of good learning. There is a need to support a diversity of positive learning experiences, as well as recognising that learning can also be harmful.
3   Improving the effectiveness of learning entails modifying learning cultures, for example by increasing functional synergies and reducing dysfunctional tensions.
4   In enhancing learning cultures, 'what works' is often localised and context specific. Attempts to impose rigid standard procedures are often negative rather than positive in effect.
5   Because of item 4, improving learning in FE entails creating maximum space for localised initiative, creativity and professional judgement, and creating more synergistic cultures to support and reward such initiatives.
6   The improvement of learning requires a reflectively critical understanding at all levels of intervention: government, college, tutor and, where possible, student.

Drivers for improvement

As we have seen, learning cultures are often persistent and many of the determining influences are outside of the control of players within the education system. However, because learning cultures are partly constructed by people there is scope for some significant change through which improvements in learning can be brought about. Some of the improvements necessary in FE require wider issues of social inequality and restrictions of the labour market and employment practices to be addressed. In this project we concentrated on the potential for change inside FE. From this perspective we identified four possible drivers for the improvement of learning, i.e. four aspects or dimensions of learning cultures which are central for the transformation of learning cultures and the improvement of learning:

- student interests
- tutors' professionalism
- pedagogy
- taking a cultural view of learning.

Student interests

What students in FE want and need is very varied, between and within particular courses. Their FE experience is not simply about passing qualifications and getting a good job – though these were goals for many. Students want to enjoy their learning, and to be able to balance their studies with other personal priorities, be that economic survival, supporting a family, doing an existing job, or sustaining a vibrant lifestyle. To operationalise this force for improvement requires the acknowledgment that sometimes students legitimately want things that policy does not support. It is also necessary to challenge student assumptions and expectations as part of the educative process.

Tutors' professionalism

We found dedicated staff, determined to do an excellent job, often in difficult conditions. If this reservoir of tutor experience, altruism and professionalism were recognised and supported, major improvements in learning would follow. This would entail creating more space for tutor autonomy and collaboration, encouraging, rewarding, sustaining and supporting creativity, imagination and innovation, and providing better tutor learning opportunities, including challenging expectations and assumptions. Tutors need more expansive learning environments at work, including opportunities to step outside the working context and engage with critical thinking – for example through engagement in research or other HE-linked courses and activities.

Pedagogy

Our data supports the view of teaching as an art rather than a technical craft. Though there are some common features of good pedagogy that can be applied almost anywhere, the nature of that application differs significantly between different sites and their learning cultures. Often the good pedagogy we observed did not completely fit the criteria set out for national standards and inspection, and what worked well for one tutor in one site might not have worked for a different tutor, or in a different site. A greater understanding of and support for excellent pedagogy that is particular to a tutor's personal approach and professional judgement and that is sensitive to the nature of the particular learning culture, should be combined with staff development that encourages critical friendship and sharing of expertise (see also Fielding 1999).

Taking a cultural view of learning

Though student interests, tutors' professionalism and pedagogy all strongly influence learning, they need to be considered together with the other factors listed earlier in relation to learning cultures as a whole. Recognising and acting upon this would open up the biggest improvements in learning of all. Our analysis suggests that sites where many of the cultural influences are broadly synergistic are likely to produce more effective learning.

If it is granted that these four drivers are crucial in attempts to improve learning cultures in FE, then it follows that such attempts should be guided by the following four aims:

1   maximising student agency
2   maximising tutor professionalism
3   improving pedagogy
4   enhancing positive aspects of a learning culture.

These aims, as we will show in the next section, are therefore the cornerstones of the *Principles of Procedure for Improving Learning in FE*.

Principles of procedure for improving learning in FE

In making recommendations for improving learning in FE the TLC project faced two dilemmas. The first is that our research clearly shows that what counts as good learning varies from site to site, so that what works in one site may be inappropriate in another. Second, the way of understanding learning as the engagement in cultural practices is at odds with dominant aspects of the current policy and management culture in FE. This judges learning success against pre-specified outcomes – *retention and achievement*. The findings do not provide any ways in which those outcomes can be universally improved. Rather, they challenge the very idea that learning success in FE can be captured through measured outputs in this way (James 2005). In order to operationalise these findings, we need a different approach. This takes us back to a debate, in the early 1970s, around what was then termed the 'aims and objectives' movement of curriculum development.

Stenhouse (1975) contrasted two forms of managing development, in relation to curriculum design. They were the objectives model, where clear and identifiable outcomes could be safely predicted in advance, and the process model, where outcomes were less predictable, and where several different outcomes could all be legitimate. We take this distinction and apply it to management approaches to the improvement of learning in FE, in a different context from that where Stenhouse was working, and in a modified manner. The dominant form of learning management at the moment is a version of the objectives model. The TLC research shows that, in the context of shortage of resources, it often makes things worse. Our data is consistent with the view that learning outcomes can be varied, that they are often not distinct from the process of learning, that what counts as a suitable outcome is contested, and that many learning outcomes are likely to be judged undesirable. It follows that a process model of management may be more appropriate.

In a process model, rather than specifying the expected outcomes, we specify ongoing approaches to improving learning. That is, we specify the desired processes which, if followed, are more rather than less likely to bring about the types of improvement that are sought. This is done through linking overall aims to more specific principles of procedure. The TLC evidence suggests two different ways of constructing a table of aims and principles of procedure. The first focuses on four drivers for learning improvement: student dispositions and agency, tutor professionalism, pedagogy and cultural enrichment. The second way to classify aims and principles is through the different players who can take action. This list includes students, tutors, college management and national government and government agencies. In England, this latter group would include the DfES, the LSC, Ofsted, Lifelong Learning UK (LLUK), the QCA and a number of leading examining bodies. There are different ways in which these two approaches can be combined. What we have chosen to do, following the sense of our research, is to arrange aims in relation to each potential driver for improvement, and then cluster principles of procedure within each aim, according to the key players who could take action. In some cases the same principle occurs for more than one aim, and/or for more than one player. In each category, we commence with principles at the national level, then examine college management, then tutors and finally students. This is because, as our research shows, actions lower down the hierarchy are to a very large extent dependent upon a suitable policy and funding climate, established from above. Of course, the multitudes of players involved in learning in FE do not fall neatly into four categories. Rather, we are using those categories of policy-maker, manager, tutor and student to illustrate the range of types of action needed. In practice, what can actually be done will depend upon the specific circumstances of a player's position and role. Thus, officers of a particular awarding body have very different scope for action compared with a senior civil servant or a member of the LSC Board. Similarly, college managers vary in level and range of responsibility, and many of them are also tutors. By tutor, we include any member of staff with responsibility for working with students, including the growing army of paraprofessionals.

In understanding the principles of procedure, two things should be kept in mind. The first is that issues of learning value and learning effectiveness are contested and contestable. This means that applying these principles of procedure is itself a contested process. Put differently, operationalising these principles entails abandoning the view that learning and the improvement of learning, are merely technical matters. Second, operationalisation has to be seen as the art of the possible. The principles are not set out as a blueprint for some unattainable idealised state. However, this does not mean that applying the principles is an inherently conservative act. Rather, for them to be effective, many aspects of the status quo must be challenged. We therefore offer the following *Principles of Procedure for Improving Learning in FE* as research-informed guidance for anyone who is serious about the improvement of learning in Further Education.

1 Maximising student agency

Aim 1: To recognise different and changing student interests in learn-
ing, and to maximise their opportunities to contribute to their own
learning.

Principles of procedure

Government and national bodies should

1.1 Continually recognise varied and diverse reasons for studying in FE, within and between different courses, as well as and instead of achieving the target qualification. This principle should guide approaches to inspection and funding, as well as guidelines for management.

1.2 Recognise and support the differing interests, aptitudes and approaches of students within and between courses. There are clear implications here for issues such as group size and teacher contact time, as well as the acceptance of varied outcomes, including for some students, leaving a course early. This principle should guide inspection, funding, curriculum design and assessment, as well as approaches to management.

1.3 Encourage colleges and tutors to recognise and support varied and changing student dispositions, even within a single course.

1.4 Encourage colleges and tutors to make sympathetic judgements about the value of diverse student dispositions and interests in learning.

In our view, taking these principles seriously entails major shifts to the management, inspection and especially resourcing of the FE sector. Catering effectively for diverse student dispositions requires time, expertise, space and support.

College management should

1.5 Continually recognise varied and diverse reasons for studying in FE, within and between different courses, as well as or instead of achieving the target qualification. This recognition should be reflected in management and monitoring approaches.

1.6 Encourage tutors and course teams to recognise and support the differing and changing interests and aptitudes of students, in all classes that they teach.

1.7 Encourage tutors and course teams to make sympathetic judgements about value of diverse student dispositions and interests in learning.

1.8 Provide adequate resources, including time, for the creative and innovative practices of tutors to support diverse and changing student dispositions. There are implications here for contact time and tutor workloads.

Tutors should

1.9 Make efforts to discover and understand the diverse and changing interests and dispositions of students we teach, including those that differ from qualification achievement.

1.10 Make sympathetic judgements about the range of learning processes and outcomes that can be legitimately valued and supported.

1.11 Support a wide range of different acceptable dispositions and interests, including helping students for whom the target qualification is not the major concern.

1.12 Recognise and address potentially negative effects of learning on students, and work to minimise them.

1.13 Encourage students to be proactive, creative and innovative in advancing their own learning, and encourage students to engage critically with their expectations.

Students should

1.14 Recognise and articulate the positive things that we can realistically hope to get from the course, and monitor changes in those hopes.

1.15 Look for ways to maximise the chances of realising those hopes, through our own actions, through relations with other students, and through engagement with the tutor.

1.16 Be creative and innovative in advancing our own learning, as well as that of others.

1.17 Consider the appropriateness of our hopes and actions in relation to other students and to tutors.

2 Maximising tutor professionalism

Aim 2: To recognise different tutor approaches to teaching and learning, and maximise the opportunities for increased tutor professionalism and creativity.

Principles of procedure

Government and national bodies should

2.1 Recognise, support and enhance the professionalism and creativity of all FE teaching and management staff, regardless of seniority or status.

2.2 Develop policies, with management, inspection and funding regimes that recognise and reward tutor professionalism, creativity and innovation. This should include the recognition that professionalism centres upon expert judgement-making, and that different professionals work in different learning contexts and in different ways.

2.3 Develop policies, approaches and structures that maximise the potential for tutor autonomy, combined with opportunities to learn, to share and to be constructively challenged. Challenges should cover value and purpose, as well as effectiveness.

2.4 Provide adequate resources and space for professional work by tutors, together with medium-term stability of structures, policies, regulation and funding, to encourage professionals to take a strategic view of their work.

College management should

2.5 Recognise and support diverse forms of tutor professionalism, creativity and innovation, arising from differences in tutor disposition and the contexts in which they work.

2.6 Reward tutor professionalism based on creativity, innovation and expert judgement-making.

2.7 Provide expansive working environments, where tutors can enhance their professionalism and creativity through mutual learning, exchanging experiences and meeting constructive challenges.

2.8 Recognise, develop, support and reward professionalism, creativity, innovation and judgement-making in all teaching and management staff, including part-timers, contract staff and teaching technicians.

Tutors should

2.9 Recognise, develop and challenge our own approaches to teaching and management, including our developing views about what good learning is, in ways that work for us. These might include personal reflection on practice, sharing ideas with and learning from others, seeking new challenges and going on courses.

2.10 Find ways to develop and increase our creativity, imagination, innovation and the quality of our professional judgements.

2.11 Recognise and support differing forms of professionalism in our colleagues and contribute to their development. Work with colleagues to establish a climate of professional learning, creativity, improvement and refined judgement-making.

Students should

2.12 Help tutors understand the strengths and weaknesses of their teaching, where they are receptive to such inputs.

2.13 Respond creatively to learning opportunities and teacher activity.

2.14 Be politely assertive, if aspects of the learning experience fall short of our needs, while striving to understand the constraints within which we and the tutors have to work.

2.15 Expect individual tutors to work in different ways, while expecting and encouraging each one to do what they can to improve our learning.

3 Improving pedagogy

Of the four drivers of potential learning improvement, this is the one that already gets most attention. In what follows, therefore, we have concentrated on a small number of more macro principles of procedure, rather than following so many others in trying to pin down the detail of good teaching approaches. This is because the TLC research shows that effective pedagogy varies significantly from learning culture to learning culture, and from tutor to tutor.

Aim 3: To improve the value and effectiveness of learning, through the pedagogic practices of tutors.

Principles of procedure

Government and national bodies should

3.1 Recognise that pedagogy involves value judgements and creativity as well as techniques, and develop systems to encourage and support the identification of a wide range of learning outcomes and processes, together with judgements about their worth, at local as well as at national levels.

3.2 Facilitate debate about what forms 'good' learning can take, and construct policies and management structures to recognise and encourage diverse forms of good learning (outcomes and processes), while supporting colleges and staff in minimising less positive forms of learning.

3.3 Recognise and support pedagogic practices that enhance and maintain a values-driven and effective learning culture in any learning site (see below). This entails widening the currently accepted range of 'good' pedagogical approaches, and recognising that what works for one tutor in one site may not work for another, in a different site.

3.4 Recognise and support tutors in developing pedagogic practices that are creative, innovative and appropriate given their dispositions and the learning culture of the sites where they work.

College management should

3.5 Recognise and help staff to recognise the importance of evaluating the value and purposes of learning, as well as its effectiveness. This entails accepting that in any learning site there will be multiple learning processes and outcomes, rather than a single one (such as achieving qualification success).

3.6 Support tutors and managers in understanding the learning cultures of the sites where they teach, and in identifying ways in which they could creatively further enhance the positive aspects of those cultures.

3.7 Develop and support a reflectively creative and critical approach to pedagogy, in opposition to views that teaching consists of a battery of universal standard techniques.

3.8 Develop and support expansive working environments, where tutors can improve their pedagogy through mutual learning, exchanging experiences and meeting constructive challenges.

3.9 Develop reward structures for tutors who are innovative, critical and reflective practitioners.

Tutors should

3.10 Identify and evaluate the range of learning processes and outcomes in any site. This entails recognising a range of positive outcomes, and that some learning can be harmful.

3.11 Develop a creative and reflectively critical approach to our own pedagogy, which takes a broad view of what we do and what we should strive to achieve. This may usefully entail seeing pedagogy as concerned with maintaining and enhancing positive learning cultures.

3.12 Work with colleagues to establish expansive learning environments for our mutual benefit. Where practicable, this would usefully entail working together to continually improve our practices, and to share judgement-making.

3.13 Where practicable, work to engage students in the processes of learning in a site. This may include encouraging students to take creative pedagogic actions for the benefit of themselves and the group.

Students should

3.14 Look for ways to be creative and innovative in supporting our own learning processes, and those of fellow students in the group.

3.15 Critically reflect on the learning of ourselves and of our fellow students, and of the parts we play in enhancing or inhibiting such learning.

4 Enhancing positive aspects of a learning culture

This is the most significant finding of the TLC research. It entails seeing the learning culture of a site as complex, relational, and greater than the sum of the parts.

Aim 4: To enhance the appropriateness and effectiveness of learning cultures in FE, and to maximise positive as opposed to negative learning processes and outcomes.

All the principles of procedure already listed contribute to this aim. What follows are important additional principles.

Principles of procedure

Government and national bodies should

4.1 Recognise that the impact of policy, management, funding and inspection approaches can have negative as well as positive effects on learning, and critically evaluate current and future approaches from this perspective.

4.2 Develop policies and management, funding and inspection approaches that enhance the learning culture of the FE sector as a whole, and encourage further enhancement at college and teaching group levels.

4.3 Recognise the impact of wider social and economic structures and processes on learning in FE, and develop policies to minimise the harmful effects of social inequalities and status hierarchies.

4.4 Encourage local responsibility and decision-making about learning, and provide the space, stable funding and support for that to take place, and for the quality of local management to be improved.

4.5 Address and minimise dysfunctional tensions and contradictions between the factors that impact upon learning in FE.

4.6 Recognise and support a range of acceptable learning processes and outcomes, reflecting the diversity of local experiences and of student needs.

College management should

4.7 Recognise that management approaches can have negative as well as positive effects upon learning, and critically evaluate current and future approaches from that perspective.

4.8 Develop policies and management approaches that enhance the learning culture of the college as a whole, and encourage further enhancement by teaching groups and individual tutors.

4.9 Encourage and facilitate local responsibility and decision-making about learning, involving creativity, imagination, innovation and professional judgement. Provide the space, stable funding and support for that to take place, within teams and by individual tutors.

4.10 Address and minimise dysfunctional tensions and contradictions between the factors that impact upon learning in the college.

4.11 Recognise and support a range of acceptable learning processes and outcomes, reflecting the diversity of specific course or group experiences and of student needs.

Tutors should

4.12 Identify the key factors affecting learning in each learning site, looking for dysfunctional tensions, constructive synergies, and areas where we have the power to make constructive changes.

4.13 Work to improve the effectiveness of learning by maximising positive synergies, and proactively and creatively influencing and mediating the learning culture.

4.14 Recognise a range of positive and negative learning processes and outcomes in any learning culture, and work to maximise the former. There are likely to be implications for recruitment and student support, as well as pedagogy.

4.15 Work collaboratively with colleagues, to enhance the learning cultures in the range of sites where we all teach, and to influence the learning culture of the college.

Students should

4.16 Work collaboratively with fellow students and tutors to enhance the culture for learning in the sites where we study, for ourselves and for other students.

Conclusion

It is sometimes assumed that good educational research will arrive at simple recipes that practitioners, policy-makers, managers and others can simply adopt. We would argue that such a view commonly under-estimates the complexity of everyday life in order to conform to a common-sense portrayal of the relationship of research and practice. The Transforming Learning Cultures in Further Education project sought continually to face up to the complexity of practice, seeing this as necessary in honouring its commitment (and that of the Teaching and Learning Research Programme of which it was part) to the study of *authentic* settings and practices.

It is important, then, not to read this chapter as some sort of complete account of the outcomes of the project, and it has to be taken together with the earlier chapters of this book, which offer a gateway to a range of other findings. The findings set out here are those that can be expressed as general principles and drivers for improvement, and also as a series of principles of procedure for the actions of four groups of key players.

Many of the principles will chime, to a greater or lesser degree, with the current perceptions of those key players, but we would suggest that to read them just for recognition (asking perhaps 'Do I agree with this or not?) is actually to miss the point, for two reasons. First, having been produced though a rigorous research process, the principles represent dependable starting-points for action, to be realised in a variety of current circumstances and constraints, and they are geared to what we think is achievable in the current climate of FE. Yet as our research has shown us all too clearly, even small improvements can be difficult or impossible to realise in this current climate. Second, though, the pragmatic flavour of the *principles* means that they cannot encapsulate all the arguments and analyses that the project has produced about change-for-the-better. Several of the analyses in our published project outputs point to a need for much more radical changes, and in such cases, changing the learning culture for the better requires transforming or disrupting some of the social relationships – between colleges, employers, government agencies and so forth – that make up the field of FE. Improving learning and teaching in FE is thus not limited to the transformation of the immediate, visible aspects but requires transformation of elements of the learning culture that go well beyond the learning site.

Methodological appendix

Introduction

The Transforming Learning Cultures in FE project was an interpretive study of learning cultures in Further Education. As we have shown in the main part of this book, using the theoretical tools of Bourdieu and others, we have explored the complexity of the relationships between teaching, teachers, learning, learners, learning situations, and wider historical, economic, social and political influences. The purpose of this appendix is to provide more detail about how this was done, to outline some of the problems that we have tried to overcome, and to indicate some of the opportunities that the project provided for innovative work.

The overarching aim of the project was to deepen understanding of the complexities of learning in FE while identifying, implementing and evaluating strategies for the improvement of that learning. It also sought to add to research capacity in FE.

The main project objectives were:

*   to determine the nature of learning cultures and their impact on students' and teachers' learning in FE
*   to establish a theoretical base for understanding the interrelationships between learning cultures, learning and situational and motivational factors in FE
*   to identify principles of procedure for the enhancement of learning cultures in order to improve student learning and achievement
*   to determine the effectiveness, within prescribed limits, of different intervention strategies for the enhancement of learning cultures and the improvement of learning

Authored by Keith Postlethwaite

- to set in place an enhanced and lasting practitioner-based research capacity in FE.

To achieve these aims and objectives, the project was structured as a set of nested case studies. We worked in four partnerships, each involving a university and a college of Further Education. The colleges served very different catchment areas in different parts of England, giving opportunities to identify the impact of the broad structural features of Further Education in England on learning, and also to reveal the impact of particular local circumstances.

In the FE college of each partnership, we studied four 'learning sites': i.e. locations where students and tutors worked together on learning. Our overall set of learning sites (see Chapter 1 for a list of the nineteen sites that were included in the research) cannot be considered to be representative of FE in any formal sense. However, they were chosen to cover as wide a range of learning situations and circumstances as possible, so that the project could be informed by, and could hope to have impact on, a substantial part of the Further Education enterprise.

In each site, data was collected through repeated interviews with a sample of (usually) six students, through interviews with the tutors who had the main teaching responsibility for the site (known as 'participating tutors'), through participating tutor journals, and through observation of the site in action. A questionnaire was also used with all the students in each site (not just the interviewees). This was administered at the start of each academic year, and at the end of the year (or at the point at which the student left the site). Thus we had data at the start and end of the site for one-year sites (or sites that students entered and left in less than a year) and data at the start, mid-point, and end for two-year sites. Where possible, exit interviews were conducted with students after they had left the site.

Data was collected for up to three consecutive cohorts of students. The overall design is summarised in Annexe 1.

To address our first and second objectives, we used the data to construct an understanding of the learning culture of each site. Exploration of similarities and differences among groups of sites, and of changes in sites over time, contributed to this construction. The third and fourth objectives were met mainly by identifying changes in the sites, and by relating these changes to external influences on the site, to influences from within the college and the site itself that were responses to changing circumstances and not specifically designed to improve the learning culture of the site, and to deliberate steps taken by the tutor to improve that learning culture. Feedback to the participating tutors about insights gained from the project enabled some of the deliberate steps they took to be based on findings from our research. In relation to these deliberate steps taken by participating tutors, the project had elements of an action research design, though it was not limited to the exploration of this kind of change and was therefore able to show both the potential, and the limitations, of conceptualising the improvement of learning in terms of actions that can be taken by tutors.

The project was centred on the work of the college tutors who had the main teaching responsibility for each of the learning sites. These participating tutors were each 'bought out' of two hours per week of their teaching so that they could contribute to the project by attending meetings with the rest of the research team in their college about all aspects of the project, providing interviews, being observed, observing other tutors' sites, keeping a research log and making innovations in their teaching as the research progressed. In each partnership, the main data collection and analysis activity was carried out by a 0.5 full-time equivalent (fte) university-based research fellow, and a 0.4 fte college-based research fellow working with a project director who was an established member of staff of the relevant university spending, nominally, one day a week on the project. In each case, the college-based research fellow was seconded to the project from the staff of the FE college. The full involvement of college-based research fellows in all aspects of the project, and the detailed work done by and with participating tutors, gave us potential to set in place an enhanced and lasting practitioner-based research capacity in FE, though one finding of the project is that it is far from easy to fulfil this potential.

Sample details

Sites

An obvious and necessary criterion for choice of site was the willingness of the tutor to be involved in the project. Within this constraint, sites were chosen to ensure variety in terms of factors such as their focus as vocational or academic programmes, and the age range, educational experience and qualifications, and social background of their students. We also sought variety in terms of how sites worked: some were one- or two-year courses, some were provision which students entered and left according to need, sometimes spending quite short periods in the site. We also chose sites that differed in relation to the location of the learning: for some sites this was a college classroom or workshop where the group of students met for lessons; for others, it was far more diffuse. For example, in some sites students came individually to IT skills sessions with their tutor, or met their tutor individually in their own workplace, or in virtual space as participants in an e-learning programme. It was for this reason that the term 'learning site' was preferred to the more usual term 'course': it reminded us that some sites had little sense of a course of study.

The full list of sites can be found in Chapter 1. Our sample clearly lacks sites in which FE makes HE provision, and has only limited engagement with sites emphasising the learning of crafts. There is some emphasis on new kinds of provision, which perhaps reflects the interest of the tutors and their colleges to investigate these new ways of working. However, our sites do encompass a wide range of FE activity. This increases the chance of capturing important insights into different aspects of FE. Also, any issues that emerge consistently across such a set of sites might be seen as having importance for FE as a whole, providing insights that could be transferred to, and thoughtfully reinterpreted in, other FE settings. While we did intend to produce ideas that would have widespread application through such a process of thoughtful transfer, it is important to stress that we did not seek to make claims for statistical generalisation of our findings to a population. Therefore, while we acknowledge that our sites are not statistically representative of any formal population of FE activity, we do not see this as a threat to the value of our work.

Students

Using data from the questionnaire surveys, which related to all students in the sites, it is possible to give general pictures of our student sample for each cohort. Tables which support these pictures are presented in Annexe 2. National data with which general comparisons are made can be found at the Learning and Skills Council (2005) website. The picture related to Cohort 3 differs somewhat from those for Cohort 1 (C1) and Cohort 2 (C2), as data was collected only on one-year sites and the CACHE site for Cohort 3 (C3).

It is important to stress again that, as in relation to our site sample, we are not claiming statistical generalisation of our findings to a wider population of FE students. Our purpose in revealing the relationship between our sample and national statistics is to alert readers to the kinds of FE sites where the students are similar to ours and to which our findings might be quite directly transferable, and to other sites where the students differ and where particular care might be needed in considering how, if at all, our findings might be applied.

Generally, our sample contained rather more full-time students than is the case nationally (C1: 54 per cent; C2: 62 per cent; C3: 88 per cent; national – all three years – 23 per cent), and rather more students in the 14–19 age group (C1: 44 per cent; C2: 61 per cent; C3: 62 per cent; national – all three years – 17 per cent). Our sample contained fewer than expected older, part-time students. The views of this kind of student may therefore have been under-represented in the interview data. Though their voice was not entirely absent, the under-representation of their views may have affected the ways in which we chose to interpret our data. Readers who are especially concerned with older part-time students might argue that some of our findings do not apply to them at the level of detail, but should still consider whether the broader outcomes of our project (for example, our concept of a learning culture, or our principles of procedure) have application to their areas of interest.

In relation to the full-time/part-time distinction, it is perhaps important to note that although students can be classified as full-time or part-time, sites cannot. In each cohort, between two and four sites contained a significant mix of full-time and part-time students, and some sites were predominantly of one kind with one or two students of the other kind also involved.

In terms of gender, our sample in Cohorts 1 and 2 were quite a close match to national data (C1: 64 per cent female; C2: 61 per cent female; national – all three years – 60 per cent female). The Cohort 3 sample was somewhat weighted towards female students (74 per cent female).

There was wide variation in the gender make-up of the sites, which ranged between predominantly male, and exclusively female, with a spread of proportions in between. There did seem to be some stereotypical sites at the extreme ends. No sites were exclusively male, but the Engineering day release site came very close. The Pathways for Parents and Health Studies BTEC sites were exclusively female.

Data on ethnicity was collected using the framework set out by the DfEE but we also allowed students the opportunity to define their ethnicity in their own terms should they wish to do so.

Our sample was largely White British (Cohort 1: 80 per cent; Cohort 2: 71 per cent; Cohort 3: 70 per cent). Directly comparable national figures for Cohort 1 were not available, but the national figures for the later cohorts were: Cohort 2: 74 per cent White British; Cohort 3: 75 per cent White British.

In Cohort 1, except in the site which offered English for Speakers of Other Languages, approximately 60 per cent or more of students were White British. In four sites, all students were White British. These four sites were located in three of the four colleges. Other sites in two of these three colleges were very mixed, suggesting that the ethnic composition of sites (like the gender composition discussed above) was a reflection of site culture, not just of the ethnic mix of the surrounding area. Although there was some variation in the ethnic mix of sites from cohort to cohort, this general picture was fairly stable.

Our questionnaire also gave insights into other aspects of students' backgrounds, aspects that are not covered in national statistics. Between 53 per cent and 66 per cent of students were living with their parents, these percentages perhaps reflecting the high proportions of students below the age of 19 in our samples. Consistent with this was the fact that only about one-third of students (C1: 31 per cent; C2: 31 per cent; C3: 39 per cent) had responsibility for others (e.g. children or older relatives).

For most students, their last experience of formal education was the year before beginning their programme in the FE college, though for a significant minority this last experience was ten or more years earlier.

We asked students about the number of hours they worked each week, paid or unpaid. The distribution for each cohort was bimodal, significant numbers doing no paid or unpaid work, and significant numbers doing eleven hours a week or more. Few students did between one and ten hours' work a week.

For Cohorts 2 and 3 we collected data on parents' highest level of education. In both cases the modal response was 'below O level'; the next highest response category in each cohort was degree level.

In Cohort 1 there was no site in which there was a significant difference between students interviewed and those not interviewed, in terms of mode of study, age, or gender; in relation to the timing of students' most recent experience of education only one site reached significance – in the photography site the interviewees were more likely to have had educational experience in the last year than were students in the site as a whole. In Cohort 2 there was only one significant difference: males were under-represented in the interview sample in the GNVQ Business Studies site. Overall, these findings suggest that the interviewees were not distinctly different from the rest of the students in the sites in terms of these basic demographics.

Data collection procedures

This section describes our approach to the collection of data through interviews, reflective journals, observation, and student questionnaire. Semi-structured interviews with students and with participating tutors were a key part of our data collection strategy. At early whole team meetings we discussed the ways in which our theoretical stance should influence the kinds of issues to be explored in the interviews, and outlined what the interview schedules should contain. These schedules were then developed to suit the context of each partnership in local team meetings. An example of the student interview schedules produced through this process is provided in Annexe 3. Common themes ran through all the interviews (for example, concern with the influence of significant others on decision-making and attitudes, views on life outside college and the student's future expectations and aspirations) though these were focused somewhat differently at different stages of the student's college career. Other issues were directly focused on the stage that the student had reached when the particular interview was conducted. Interviews were tape recorded and fully transcribed.

As well as being interviewed regularly, participating tutors were encouraged to keep a professional journal. The team provided guidance for this. Again, the framework was discussed in a whole team meeting, using insights from existing literature such as Holly (1984); local teams then developed detailed guidance for their group of participating tutors. As well as giving indications of the purpose of the journals for the research, and outlining such things as what might be included and when journals might be written, the guidance also alerted participating tutors to the fact that writing a journal can generate feelings of vulnerability and can be challenging, but can also be an exciting source of stimulus for professional development. Tutors were assured that although the TLC researchers would hope to be given access to journal content for the purposes of the project, the participating tutor would always be in control of what was shared.

This process for the development of interview schedules and journal guidance was deliberately designed by the project team. Given our view of the situated nature of learning and the weight we gave to the Bourdieusian perspective of reflexivity discussed in Part II, we argued that it was essential for local teams to have control over the details of their data collection procedures within general agreements about the overall purpose and broad structure of those procedures. We acknowledged that this would give rise to additional complexity at the level of analysis, but argued that this was an inevitable consequence of the kind of picture we wanted to produce. We therefore argued that it was better to devote time to handling that complexity rather than to try to simplify analysis by attempting to impose what would inevitably be an unproductive (and probably unworkable) uniformity across the different partnerships.

Participating tutors were observed teaching. Observing classes as part of quality assurance procedures has become a contentious matter in many FE colleges and existing practices varied in the four partner colleges. Some observations led to summative judgements about the quality of teaching and were completed by designated staff using a defined set of criteria, such as those used in Ofsted and Adult Learning Inspectorate (ALI) inspections. Some observations had an essentially diagnostic and formative role allied to staff development or teacher education. We wanted observation to serve a very different purpose, namely to give insight into what was going on in teaching sessions in the site – not to evaluate that teaching. We therefore used a wide and fluid set of questions to focus the observations and we encouraged participating tutors to take part in observing classes taught by other participating tutors. Often, observers wrote very little while observing sessions, but wrote up detailed field notes immediately afterwards. These notes were usually shared with the observed tutors and became part of the schedule for the interviews with those tutors.

To develop the questionnaire, a discussion paper was produced for consideration by the whole project team. This set out a number of areas to be covered by the instrument, and proposed some tentative questionnaire items. The meeting agreed that it was not possible directly to address some of the theoretical framework of the project (e.g. Bourdieu's notions of habitus, field and cultural capital) through a questionnaire, because even within a specific site, relevant questions could not be sufficiently contextualised to be meaningful. We argued that exploration of these ideas was the proper domain of the qualitative inquiry and that the questionnaire should provide complementary insights that could be related back to the theoretical positions of the project at the level of interpretation of findings.

We therefore argued that the questionnaire should address three broad areas. The first was general information about the students that would help us to locate them in a wider social context. We agreed to focus such questions on specific points, rather than broader constructs, such as asking about the student's employment situation and whether or not they had dependants, rather than about socio-economic status and marital status. The second broad area referred to factors affecting students' study (Cook and Leckey 1999). The relevant questions included students' perceptions of the impact on their learning of such things as time spent travelling, the attitudes of others to their study, their social life, and their own study skills. We were careful to keep open the possibility that such factors may have positive effects for some students, even though the expectation from the literature was that they would impose constraints on learning. (This section of the questionnaire was modified at the end of the first year, to explore subsequent students' views on interesting issues that arose in the free response answers given by students in Cohort 1.) Finally, the questionnaire included scales designed to assess students' perceptions of the learning environment provided by their site. Several scales were considered for use but the scale finally accepted was the Constructivist Learning Environment Survey because this most closely matched the socially constructed view of learning that was central to the project.

Once the content of the questionnaire had been decided, a letter for students was drafted explaining the purpose of the project and the place of the questionnaire within it, and a consent form was designed.

The questionnaire and its supporting documentation were piloted with students in two very different learning sites at one of the colleges. This was done before the start of the data collection for Cohort 1. One site used in the pilot involved part-time students studying for the Cert Ed FE while they were themselves teaching in FE. The other site involved full-time students studying for City and Guilds 726 – a vocational, information technology course. Since the C&G726 group contained students with learning difficulties, we felt that this opportunistic sample would give useful insights into the usefulness of the questionnaire for the full range of project sites. From this pilot study it seemed that the questionnaire was generating valid and valuable insights, that it seemed likely to be manageable for the range of students in the project, and that it was practicable in terms of the time needed to administer it effectively. Further discussion of the design and initial use of the questionnaire is available (Postlethwaite and Maull 2003).

Data analysis

The data collection processes outlined above and in Annexe 1 generated a huge amount of data that enabled us to construct rich pictures of learning cultures in FE, but which also threatened to overwhelm us. In this section, we will outline the processes we used to control the potential problems in order effectively to exploit the related opportunities.

Initially, the quantitative and qualitative data were analysed separately. They were then integrated through an iterative process, between each major sweep of data collection.

In analysing the quantitative data, our intention was to explore differences among sites, to map changes in expectations over time, to relate expectations to perceived outcomes, and to look for relationships between sets of variables. This called for use of inferential techniques including correlation, t tests, ANOVA (with post-hoc comparisons), factor analysis, and regression.

These techniques can reveal results that may be difficult to identify in other ways, and can therefore focus some aspects of the qualitative analysis. However, as we have stated several times above, it is hard to justify our samples of students and of sites as representative of any population. Generalisation of statistically significant differences or relationships is therefore problematic. Given our commitment to learning as a situated endeavour, it is also undesirable. Our response to this is to interpret our statistical findings non-inferentially (Backhouse 1984). In this approach, the $p < 0.05$ level of significance is used, not to indicate that generalisation to a population is acceptable, but simply as a consistent yardstick, for the particular group of students or sites currently being investigated, by which to separate findings worthy of further investigation and discussion from the rest. This is a particularly appropriate use of statistics in the current project, where the quantitative data serves to support and extend the findings from the qualitative strand. In this qualitative strand, results are only directly applicable to the particular sites or students at the time those data were collected. Quantitative results that meet the $p < 0.05$ criterion should therefore prompt careful study of qualitative data collected on *the same site at the same time*, so that a fuller understanding of the site can be obtained by the combination of the results of the two kinds of analysis. Just as change is to be expected in a qualitative study of a site when the students in that site change, so in this use of quantitative data, we would not be surprised by instability in the quantitative findings for the sites from one cohort of students to another. Such instability does not invalidate the findings for a particular group of students at a particular time. It may, however, alter our sense of how fundamental a particular result might be for the development of a more general understanding of the sites.

In analysing the qualitative data, we used each site as the main analytical tool. After the first round of data collection, the researchers responsible for each site produced a detailed case study account of that site. We did not produce new case studies from each round of data collection. Instead, as the project progressed, the initial case studies were updated progressively, focusing on deepening understanding, mapping change, and examining in depth the impact of various interventions into site culture – either initiated by the participating tutors, or externally imposed. For an example of such a case study, see Wahlberg and Gleeson (2003).

Participating tutors were involved in the development of the case studies of their site, but to preserve the confidentiality of the students, tutors were not given access to the interview transcripts. Instead, we discussed sites informally, and shared draft written accounts of the site. Participating tutors' comments on these drafts were treated as additional data through which the case study could be deepened. This approach recognised that participating tutors were both involved in the research and subjects of it.

Alongside these case studies we explored student perspectives (Davies and Tedder 2003), and issues of tutor professionalism (Anderson et al. 2003).

As a first step in moving beyond individual case studies, the researchers responsible for each site produced short summaries of each case study to enable the whole team to share an understanding of all the sites without being swamped by detail. Through scrutiny of these summaries, and whole team discussion based on them, we addressed some broad themes drawing on data from the project as a whole: see, for example, Colley et al. (2003b). These themes reflected the issues which emerged as important in individual case studies yet also found resonance with data produced by other members of the team.

In addition, we produced two analytical tools to enable us to address two key issues defined for the project as a whole, in the original bid to ESRC: the analysis of learning cultures and the analysis of interventions. Each instrument was designed by one project director (analysis of learning cultures: Hodkinson; analysis of interventions: James) informed by long and detailed discussions within the team at whole team meetings. Each instrument encouraged the researchers responsible for each site to search their data for insights into particular issues. The learning cultures instrument encouraged a focus on an analysis of convergences and divergences found in each site; an analysis of balance (or lack of it) within each site; an overview of each site, linked with a summary of the strengths and weaknesses of the existing learning culture; an analysis of possible ways in which the culture of each site might be transformed, setting out the costs and benefits of each approach. The interventions instrument encouraged a focus on the nature, origins and impetus for intervention in a site; the situated rationale of and/or justification for the intervention; the outcomes and consequences of the intervention; key contextual matters; the model of change (if any) held by the tutor, the manager or the students in a site. The working papers produced by the team in response to these instruments were analysed by the relevant project director and the analysis was debated by the whole team at a team meeting.

The *integration of insights from the qualitative and quantitative strands* of the project was achieved, at the simplest level, through regular comment from the researchers responsible for the quantitative work on drafts of all kinds of qualitative analysis. However, the quantitative team also explored groupings of sites, and the differences between these groupings (e.g. using ANOVA and post-hoc comparisons). We then interrogated the qualitative data for factors that helped to explain the position of a site in this analysis. It is tempting to stop such a process for a given site once a quantitative effect (such as the location of that site in a group of a particular kind) has been 'explained' by a relevant qualitative description for that site. However, if the same quantitative effect is explained in a different way for different sites, we argued that, in any of these sites, and especially for particular individuals in any of these sites, the processes involved may have been a complex inter-weaving of any or all of the explanations identified across the group of sites as a whole. As well as increasing the range of possible explanations in any one site, the whole set of explanations can lead to the recognition of a deeper level explanation. For example, a tendency for students not to discuss work with one another was explained by geographical separation in one site (they were in different work placements), by linguistic differences in another (students spoke different first languages and were not yet fluent in English), and by the structure of the sessions in two others (students came to the site individually at different times). Once we acknowledged that, at least for some students, any of these factors might have explained a lack of peer discussion in any of the sites, the nature of the factors led us to propose that the deeper construct of isolation may have been an important contributor to the learning culture of all those sites. We then checked other sites where there was significant student interaction to ensure that these did not have features of isolation, and found that they did not. By resisting the temptation to find neat, simple solutions, we moved backwards and forwards between the qualitative and quantitative strands of the project to understand the web of influences in each site as deeply as possible. This aspect of analysis is explored further by Postlethwaite and Maull (2003).

Warrants

The TLC project was positioned in the field of research in ways that suggest that it has much to offer to a wide range of audiences. It was concerned with both theoretical advancement and practical improvement, and therefore lay in 'Pasteur's quadrant' (Stokes 1997). It was strategic: although it was concerned with mapping the transformations that take place in FE as result of the impact of many different influences, it was also concerned with being one of those influences itself, and therefore with stimulating, supporting and evaluating some change. It was a project that closely fits the definition of applied and practice-based research offered by Furlong and Oancea (2005: 9): 'research conducted in, with and/or for practice'.

Furlong and Oancea (2005) suggest that the quality of practice-based educational research should be judged against four kinds of criteria (epistemic, technological, capacity development and economic) though the relevance of each may be differently weighted in different projects. We argue that the TLC project can demonstrate quality in all four areas.

Epistemic quality – a concern for methodological and theoretical robustness

The project had a clear theoretical basis and, as illustrated previously, used this consistently (though not exclusively) to structure its overall methodology and its methods of data collection and analysis. It built on this theory to generate new understandings of learning (through its cultural analysis of learning in sites) and of change (through its analysis of interventions). Its findings are therefore clearly located in a field of educational theory, and extend and deepen understanding in that field.

Ethical issues were addressed explicitly throughout the project. Given the close involvement of practitioners, great care was taken to preserve confidentiality (e.g. not sharing student interview transcripts with tutors) and to avoid breaches of anonymity, through careful use of pseudonyms, including the use of generic titles for sites that, in their own college, are known by names which are (probably) unique to that college. Explicit agreements were also established about publication (including principles for the naming of authors) and for the use of data after the end of the project.

Data were collected by researchers who understood the FE context. Repeated interviews with students and participating tutors gave opportunities for clarification of points made in earlier interviews. Within the limits imposed by the need for confidentiality for the students, descriptive summaries of the data were shared with the participating tutors, and disagreements about the picture being presented were used as additional data. Although flexibility over details of data collection and analysis was allowed (indeed, was consistent with our theoretical position), the team worked together to develop explicit guidelines that structured each of the tasks that we undertook.

On the basis of our data, we were able to locate the site and student samples within the national picture for FE (see, for example, Annexe 3) making clear which aspects of FE were well represented in our samples and which (e.g. older part-time students) were somewhat under-represented. We were able to locate our interview samples within the whole student sample in each site and therefore showed that interviewees were not (at least in broad demographic terms) outliers within their sites.

We checked the validity of the questionnaire, not only by a pilot study but also by using the main questionnaire data to paint anonymised pen pictures of interviewees and offering these to the tutors who knew the students. Tutors found that they could identify the individuals from these pen pictures.

We analysed qualitative and quantitative data separately then compared insights, finding enough synergy to suggest that findings were not artefacts of one or other method.

The development of findings was regarded as the responsibility of the whole team, comprising experienced academics with backgrounds in sociology, social psychology and philosophy, research fellows with widely differing career paths and previous interests, and college-based research fellows with a clear and ongoing connection to practice in FE. Differences of view within this team were accepted as making an important contribution to the development of the findings and were always given serious attention as our understandings were refined.

We produced detailed case studies of each site which provide rich descriptions that meet criteria of 'completeness' for the case, and for other papers that relate to that case.

From its earliest days, the project published regularly in peer reviewed journals, and reviewer comments provided wider input to the ideas as they developed. Audience participation at conference presentations in the United Kingdom and overseas served a similar function.

Technological quality – a concern for impact

This cannot be disconnected from epistemic quality. The former warrants the trustworthiness of the understandings that were (indeed, still are being) created by the project. These understandings are themselves levers for changes as 'Practices are changed by changing the ways in which they are understood' (Carr and Kemmis 1986: 91). However, there are other features of the TLC project which we argue enhances its claim to technological quality.

A difficulty highlighted by Furlong and Oancea (2005) is that the importance of a research focus and its timeliness are factors that are likely to affect its impact and yet these are often in tension as timely issues may be of only short-term importance. Our cultural model of learning is grounded in the day-to-day practice of FE tutors and the current experiences of students both inside the classroom and more generally. It is therefore centrally informed by timely issues. One consequence of the model is that it challenges much current policy in FE (e.g. its emphasis on predetermined standards of teaching quality in teacher education and inspection models), and the monitoring systems that flow from it (e.g. emphasis on such issues as retention rates). Such issues have been much more than matters of short-term importance. Further, they have resonance well beyond the FE sector. It is therefore, at the same time, centrally concerned with important issues.

A key issue in ensuring the impact of the project is the relevance and accessibility of the research to users. The fact that the project was centred on the work of participating tutors who provided data and met regularly with their local research fellows to discuss findings helped to ensure that relevance and accessibility were issues of concern as the findings were being created, not as a matter of re-presentation of those findings after the event. This was not without difficulty as the ideas we developed were not in the mainstream thinking of the practitioners and it was important not to allow issues of accessibility to limit or distort the emerging ideas. We argue that the acceptability of the findings to academics and the continued engagement of the practitioners in the research, indicates that we were able, through our intensive and extended contact with the practitioners, to reconcile these demands.

We recognised that our emerging understanding of the importance of the notion of learning cultures had implications for students, tutors, managers at all levels in colleges, policy-makers in the field of FE and government. The dissemination strategy for the project has taken this into account. By involving the Learning and Skills Development Agency, we have tested our ideas on wide FE lecturer/manager audiences and been told that our data resonated with their experience, and that our interpretation was powerful. By discussing our findings at a seminar with policy-makers from the DfES Standards Unit, we have directly involved the policy community. Feedback from these conferences and meetings has (like feedback within the team) been used to advance the ideas themselves.

Impact across this range of users cannot be immediate, but we have taken care to produce principles of procedure to highlight the implications for each kind of user of taking a cultural view of learning. These principles do not offer prescriptions for practice (something that would be anathema to our situated understanding of learning) but do provide a framework that can be used creatively and flexibly to guide the construction of practice in a given setting. Like other outputs these principles of procedure have been shared with the practitioner community at conferences.

Capacity development

The involvement of participating tutors not only as providers of data, but also as agents in the development of new practice and as collaborators in the interpretation of data, has meant that the FE tutors now have practical experience of engagement in research. Some of those participating tutors contributed sections to a formal publication outlining some of the processes and early findings of the project (James 2004). The role of college-based research fellows in all aspects of the project ensured that four FE staff are well versed in all stages of the research process including (for some) publication in peer-reviewed journals and presentation at academic and practitioner conferences. Some research fellows (especially some of the university-based research fellows) began the project with experience of research – sometimes quite extensive experience. All the research fellows have now, to understandably different degrees, demonstrated their ability to function as part of a research team. Many are clearly able to function independently as researchers.

Three university-based research fellows and one college-based research fellow have achieved a doctorate and one of the university-based research fellows has been appointed to an established post; one project director has been awarded a Chair; three research fellows have moved on to other research appointments. However, the achievements of colleagues should be seen in the context of three incidents of ill health, and lack of continuity of employment for some contract researchers.

The TLC project also indicates the difficulty of planning for capacity development in the current HE/FE context. Three of our college-based research fellows left their positions in their college during the project; one who left after the first year of the project was replaced; two who left after the second year were not replaced but continued to be involved as part-time employees. Collaborating colleges have been involved in mergers, changes in management and moves to different sites. Two of the four universities have imposed major structural changes on the departments involved in the project including significant job losses.

Economic quality

Among the research outcomes, highlights include

- the development of a cultural theory of learning
- the synthesis of cultural and interventions analyses
- two methodological innovations – integrating qualitative and quantitative approaches, and synthesising large volumes of qualitative data
- the use of a cultural theory of learning to develop new ways of understanding the enhancement of learning.

There is no doubt that these findings and other aspects of the project are 'marketable'; as well as publishing numerous journal articles and making over twenty conference presentations, we have been asked to write two special issues of journals (one already completed).

This was undoubtedly a complex project across eight institutions, a team of thirty, and a period of four years. We feel that we have demonstrated that, with the goodwill and commitment of the team, it is entirely feasible to complete such a complex project, on time and within budget, despite the fact that no one was employed full-time on the research and therefore everyone was juggling the demand of the project with the other demands of busy professional and personal lives.

Another indicator of value for money provided by the project is that the TLC project has played a significant part in the work of the ESRC TLRP programme of which it is part. TLC researchers have been members of the TLRP Learning Outcomes Thematic Group, and the TLRP Thematic Group on Lifecourse and Learning and have contributed papers to publications of both groups. The team is always fully represented at the TLRP annual conferences, and has given papers to Research Capacity Building Network (RCBN) events.

Summary

In the terms set out by M. James et al. (2005) the project meets theoretical, empirical and user warrants. It demonstrates integrity of process. Its findings are plausible to academic and user audiences. Its methods provide an explicit basis on which to transfer its findings to specific practice contexts.

Annexe 1

Cohort	Start of Yr 1	During Yr 1	End of Yr 1	Start of Yr 2	During Yr 2	End of Yr 2	Start of Yr 3	During Yr 31	End of Yr 3
1	Round 1 student interviews		Round 2 student inverviews	Round 3 student inverviews – two-year courses		Round 4 student inverviews – two-year courses			
	Entry questionnaire		Exit questionnaire – one-year courses	Continuation questionnaire – two-year courses		Exit questionnaire – two-year courses			
		Observations			Observations				
		Tutor journals			Tutor journals				
		2 Tutor interviews			2 Tutor interviews				
						Exit interviews C1 one-year courses		Exit interviews C1 two-year courses	
2				Round 1 student interviews		Round 2 student interviews	Round 3 student interviews – two-year courses		Round 4 student interviews – two-year courses
				Entry questionnaire		Exit questionnaire – one-year courses	Continuation questionnaire – two-year courses		Exit questionnaire – two-year courses
					Observations			Observations	
					Tutor journals			Tutor journals	
					2 Tutor inverviews			2 Tutor inverviews	
								Exit interviews C2 one-year courses	
3							Round 1 student inverviews – one-year sites		Round 2 student inverviews – one-year sites
							Entry questionnaire – one-year sites		Exit questionnaire – one-year sites
								Observations	
								Tutor journals	
								2 Tutor interviews	

Figure A1.1 Time-line for data collection

Annexe 2

Basic demographic information about the sample and comparable national statistics

The source for national statistics on age, mode of attendance and gender was Table 8, ILR/SFR05. National data on ethnicity were derived from Table 3 of ILR/SFR02 and Table 3 of ILR/SFR05 (LSC 2005).

Table A2.1 Mode of attendance

(i) Sample n (%)

Cohort	Full-time	Part-time
1	124 (54)	105 (46)
2	117 (62)	73 (38)
3	95 (88)	13 (12)

Each cell shows the number of respondents in that category in the sample and the percentage this represents of the total for that cohort.

(ii) National %

Cohort	Full-time	Part-time
1	23	77
2	22	78
3	23	77

Each cell shows the percentage of the total for that cohort.

Table A2.2 Age

(i) Sample n

Cohort	<16	17–18	19–21	22–25	26–35	36–50	51+
1	46	55	47	22	27	26	6
2	63	53	24	15	20	10	4
3	26	41	10	8	11	10	3

Table A2.2 continued

(ii) Sample %

Cohort	<19	19+
1	44	56
2	61	39
3	62	38

(iii) National %

Cohort	<19	19+
1	17	82
2	16	83
3	17	83

In each year, national statistics have 1% of cases 'age unknown'.

Table A2.3 Gender

(i) Sample: n (%)

Cohort	Male	Female
1	82 (36)	147 (64)
2	74 (39)	117 (61)
3	28 (26)	81 (74)

(ii) National %

Cohort	Male	Female
1	41	59
2	40	60
3	40	60

Table A2.4 Ethnicity

Sample n

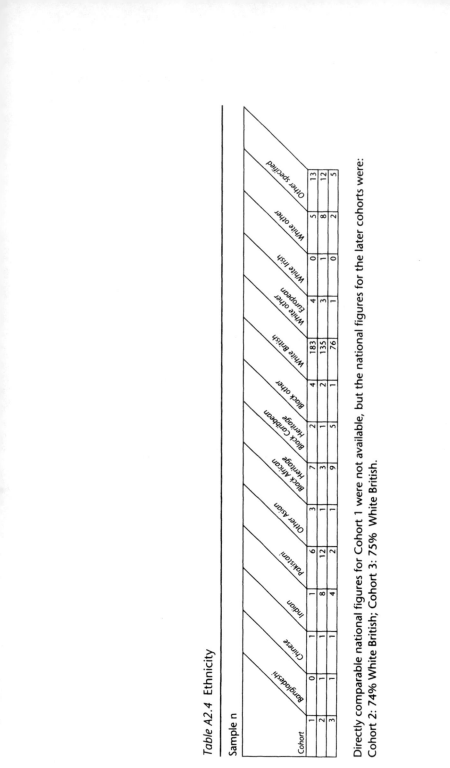

Cohort	Bangladeshi	Chinese	Indian	Pakistani	Other Asian	Black African Heritage	Black Caribbean Heritage	Black other	White British	White other European	White Irish	White other	Other specified
1	0	1	1	6	3	7	2	4	183	4	0	5	13
2	1	1	8	12	1	3	1	2	135	3	1	8	12
3	1	1	4	2	1	9	5	1	76	1	0	2	5

Directly comparable national figures for Cohort 1 were not available, but the national figures for the later cohorts were: Cohort 2: 74% White British; Cohort 3: 75% White British.

Additional background information on the sample, not covered in national statistics

Raw numbers are given in each table.

Table A2.5 Living arrangements

Cohort	Shared	On own	Parents	Partner	Other
1	24	24	122	42	17
2	13	16	126	31	3
3	12	14	67	14	2

Table A2.6 Last educational experience

Cohort	Last year	2–5 yrs ago	6–9 yrs ago	10+ yrs ago
1	166	37	10	14
2	138	40	4	6
3	74	14	5	6

Table A2.7 Responsibility for others?

Cohort	No	Yes
1	159	70
2	138	59
3	67	42

Table A2.8 Hours of work per week (paid or unpaid)

Cohort	0	1–5	6–10	11–20	21+
1	74	13	19	50	55
2	29	14	10	37	49
3	17	6	13	24	10

Table A2.9 Highest parental education

Cohort	Below O level	O level	A level	Degree
2	107	20	22	43
3	71	6	7	20

(Data not available for Cohort 1)

Annexe 3

An example of interview outlines for students on two-year courses in one HE/FE partnership; italicised items are those that were revisited in interviews.

First interview (main focus: starting at college and biography)

- initial impressions of college and course
- previous education
- family
- *influence of significant others in decision-making/attitudes*
- *life outside college*
- *future expectations and aspirations.*

Second interview (main focus: the course)

- knowledge
- 'motivation' – being a student
- describing learning situations – what 'works'/'doesn't work'
- group dynamics
- relationship with tutor
- coping with assignments/exams/work placements
- *influence of significant others in decision-making/attitudes*
- *life outside college*
- *future expectations and aspirations.*

Third interview (main focus: second year of course compared with first year)

- significant events over the summer
- being a 'good' student
- changes from last year re teaching/learning
- qualifications (including parental qualifications)
- work experience
- vocational aspirations – including gender issues; career compared with job
- *influence of significant others in decision-making/attitudes*
- *life outside college* – especially part-time employment
- *the future* and 'becoming adult'.

Fourth interview (main focus: finishing the course)

- comparisons re teaching/learning with other stages in course
- comparisons with initial expectations
- 'good' teacher
- enthusiasm and interest
- 'success' on course
- effect(s) of interventions – both tutor and external
- leaving college (school)
- going to work/future study
- important values/individuals
- *influence of significant others in decision-making/attitudes*
- *life outside college*
- *the future.*

Fifth (exit) interview (main focus: looking back/forwards)

- major changes in life since leaving college
- effect(s) of college experience (learning issues)
- current situation – employment, study etc.
- most important aspects of life at present
- *future aspirations – near future*
- *future aspirations – longer term*
- *influence of significant others in decision-making/attitudes*
- experience of taking part in TLC project.

References

Ainley, P. and Bailey, B. (1997) *The Business of Learning: Staff and student experiences of Further Education in the 1990s*, London: Cassell.

Anderson, G., Barton, S. and Wahlberg, M. (2003) 'Reflections and experiences of Further Education research in practice', *Journal of Vocational Education and Training* 55(4): 499–516.

Apple, M. and Jungck, S. (1991) 'You don't have to be a teacher to teach in this unit: teaching, technology and control in the classroom', in A. Hargreaves and M. Fullan (eds) *Understanding Teacher Development*, London: Cassell.

Archer, M. (2003) *Structure, Agency and the Internal Conversation*, Cambridge: Cambridge University Press.

Armitage, A., Bryant, R., Dunnill, R., Hammersley, M., Hayes, D., Hudson, A. and Lawes, S. (1999) *Teaching and Training in Post-compulsory Education*, Buckingham: Open University Press.

Ashcroft, K. and James, D. (1999) *The Creative Professional*, London: Falmer Press.

Avis, J. (1983) 'ABC and the new vocational consensus', *Journal of Further and Higher Education* 7(1): 23–33.

Avis, J., Bloomer, M., Esland, G., Gleeson, D. and Hodkinson, P. (1996) *Knowledge and Nationhood: Education, politics and work*, London: Cassell.

Avis, J., Bathmaker, A-M. and Parsons, J. (2002) 'Communities of practice and the construction of learners in post-compulsory education and training', *Journal of Vocational Education and Training* 54(1): 27–50.

Backhouse, J.K. (1984) 'Inferential and non-inferential tests', *Educational Research* 26(1): 52–55.

Ball, S.J. (2005) 'Education reform as social barbarism: economism and the end of authenticity', The SERA Lecture 2004, *Scottish Educational Review* 37(1): 4–16.

Bates, I. (1990) 'No bleeding, whining Minnies: the role of YTS in class and gender reproduction', *British Journal of Education and Work* 3(2): 91–110.

Bates, I. (1991) 'Closely observed training: an exploration of links between social structures, training and identity', *International Studies in Sociology of Education* 1: 225–243.

Bates, I. (1994) 'A job which is "Right for me"? Social class, gender and indi-
vidualization', in I. Bates and G. Riseborough (eds) *Youth and Inequality*,
Buckingham: Open University Press.

Bathmaker, A-M. (2001) 'Neither dupes nor devils: teachers' constructions of
their changing role in further education', paper presented at the Fifth Annual
Conference of the Learning and Skills Research Network, Robinson College,
University of Cambridge, December.

Bathmaker, A-M., Avis, J., Kendall, A. and Parsons, J. (2002) 'Biographies, values
and practice: trainee lecturers' constructions of teaching in Further
Education', paper presented at the Annual Conference of the British
Educational Research Association, University of Exeter, September. Available
at http://www.leeds.ac.uk/educol/documents/00002379.htm (accessed
April 2007).

Biesta, G.J.J. (1994) 'Education as practical intersubjectivity: towards a critical-
pragmatic understanding of education', *Educational Theory* 44(3): 299–317.

Biesta, G.J.J. (1995) 'Pragmatism as a pedagogy of communicative action', in
J. Garrison (ed.) *The New Scholarship on John Dewey*, Dordrecht: Kluwer.

Biesta, G.J.J. (1999) 'Redefining the subject, redefining the social, reconsidering
education: George Herbert Mead's course on Philosophy of Education at the
University of Chicago', *Educational Theory* 49(4): 475–492.

Biesta, G.J.J. (2001) 'How difficult should education be?', *Educational Theory*
51(4): 385–400.

Biesta, G.J.J. (2004a) 'Against learning; reclaiming a language for education in
an age of learning', *Nordisk Pedagogik* 23: 70–82.

Biesta, G.J.J. (2004b) 'Education, accountability and the ethical demand: can
the democratic potential of accountability be regained?', *Educational Theory*
54(3): 233–250.

Biesta, G.J.J. (2004c) '"Mind the gap!" Communication and the educational
relation', in C. Bingham and A.M. Sidorkin (eds) *No Education without
Relation*, New York: Peter Lang.

Biesta, G.J.J. (2006) *Beyond Learning: Democratic education for a human future*,
Boulder, CO: Paradigm.

Biesta, G.J.J. (2007) 'Why "what works" won't work: evidence-based practice and
the democratic deficit of educational research', *Educational Theory* 57(1): 1–22.

Biesta, G.J.J. and Burbules, N.C. (2003) *Pragmatism and Educational Research*,
Lanham, MD: Rowman & Littlefield.

Bloomer, M. (1997) *Curriculum Making in Post-16 Education: The social conditions of studentship*, London: Routledge.

Bloomer, M. (1998) 'They tell you what to do and then they let you get on with
it: illusions of progressivism in GNVQ', *Journal of Education and Work* 11:
167–186.

Bloomer, M. and Hodkinson, P. (2000) 'Learning careers: continuity and change
in young people's dispositions to learning', *British Educational Research
Journal* 26: 583–598.

Bloomer, M. and Hodkinson, P. (2002) 'Learning careers and cultural capital: adding a social and longitudinal dimension to our understanding of learning', in R. Nata (ed.) *Progress in Education*, Vol. 5, Hauppauge, NY: Nova Science.

Bloomer, M. and James, D. (2003) 'Educational research in educational practice', *Journal of Further and Higher Education* 27(3): 247–256.

Blunkett, D. (2000) 'Influence or irrelevance: can social science improve government'? Secretary of State's Economic and Social Research Council Lecture, London: Economic and Social Research Council/Department for Education and Employment, 2 February.

Bourdieu, P. (1977) *Outline of a Theory of Practice*, Cambridge: Cambridge University Press.

Bourdieu, P. (1984) *Distinction: A social critique of the judgement of taste*, London: Routledge.

Bourdieu, P. (1989) 'Towards a reflexive sociology: a workshop with Pierre Bourdieu', *Sociological Theory* 7: 26–63.

Bourdieu, P. (1990) *The Logic of Practice*, Cambridge: Polity Press.

Bourdieu, P. (1996) *The Rules of Art*, Cambridge: Polity Press.

Bourdieu, P. (1998) *Practical Reason*, Cambridge: Polity Press.

Bourdieu, P. and Wacquant, L.J.D. (1992) *An Invitation to Reflexive Sociology*, Cambridge: Polity Press.

Bourn, J. (2001) *Improving Student Performance: How English FE colleges can improve student retention and achievement*, London: National Audit Office, Stationery Office.

Brown, J.S., Collins, A. and Duguid, P. (1989) 'Situated cognition and the culture of learning', *Educational Researcher* 18(1): 32–42.

Brown, M. and James, M. (2005) 'Grasping the TLRP nettle: preliminary analysis and some enduring issues surrounding the improvement of learning outcomes', *The Curriculum Journal* 16(1): 7–30.

Bruner, J. (1996) *The Culture of Education*, London: Harvard University Press.

Campbell, R.J. and Neill, S.R.St.J. (1994) *Secondary Teachers at Work*, London: Routledge.

Carey, J.W. (1992) *Communication as Culture: Essays on media and society*, New York: Routledge.

Carr, W. and Kemmis, S. (1986) *Becoming Critical*, London: Falmer Press.

Coffield, F. (ed.) (2000) *Differing Visions of the Learning Society*, Vol. 1, Bristol: Policy Press.

Coffield, F., Moseley, D., Hall, E. and Ecclestone, K. (2004) *Learning Styles and Pedagogy in Post-16 Learning: A systematic and critical review*, London: Learning and Skills Research Council.

Colley, H. (2003) *Mentoring for Social Inclusion: A critical approach to nurturing mentor relationships*, London: RoutledgeFalmer.

Colley, H. (2006) 'Learning to labour with feeling: class, gender and emotion in childcare education and training', *Contemporary Issues in Early Childhood* 7(1): 15–29.

Colley, H., Hodkinson, P. and Malcolm, J. (2003a) *Informality and Formality in Learning: A report for the Learning and Skills Research Centre*, London: Learning and Skills Research Centre.

Colley, H., James, D., Tedder, M. and Diment, K. (2003b) 'Learning as becoming in vocational education and training: class, gender and the role of vocational habitus', *Journal of Vocational Education and Training* 55(4): 471–497.

Colley, H., James, D. and Diment, K. (2007) 'Unbecoming tutors? Towards a more dynamic notion of professional participation', *Journal of Education Policy* 22(2): 173–193.

Cook, A. and Leckey, J. (1999) 'Do expectations meet reality: a survey of changes in first year students' opinions', *Journal of Further and Higher Education* 23(2): 157–171.

Crowther, G. (1959) *15–18: A report of the Central Advisory Council for Education (England)*, London: HMSO.

Curzon, L.B. (2004) *Teaching in Further Education: An outline of principles and practice*, 6th edn, London: Continuum.

Davies, J. and Tedder, M. (2003) 'Becoming vocational: insights from two vocational courses in a further education college', *Journal of Vocational Education and Training* 55(1): 517–539.

Department for Education and Employment (DfEE) (1998) *The Learning Age: A Renaissance for a new Britain*, London: Stationery Office.

Department for Education and Employment (DfEE) (1999) *Learning to Succeed: A new framework for post-16 learning*, London: Stationery Office.

Department for Education and Employment (DfEE) (2000) *Statistics of Education: Schools in England*, Norwich: Stationery Office.

Department of Education and Science (DES) (1977) *Education in Schools: A consultative document*, London: HMSO.

Department for Education and Skills (DfES) (2003a) *21st Century Skills: Realizing our potential*, London: Stationery Office.

Department for Education and Skills (DfES) (2003b) *The Future of Initial Teacher Education for the Learning and Skills Sector: An agenda for reform*, Standards Unit consultation paper, London: DfES.

Department for Education and Skills (DfES) (2006) *Further Education: Raising skills, improving life chances*, Norwich: Stationery Office.

Dewey, J. (1957[1922]) *Human Nature and Conduct: An introduction to social psychology*, New York: The Modern Library.

Dewey, J. (1963[1938]) *Experience and Education*, New York: Collier.

Dewey, J. (1990[1902; 1900]) *The School and Society and The Child and the Curriculum*, Chicago, IL: University of Chicago Press.

Diment, K. (2005) '"Though this be madness, yet there is method in't" – using drama as methodological research tool', paper presented at Discourses of Difference Seminar Series, Institute of Education, University of London.

Ecclestone, K. (2002) *Learning Autonomy in Post-16 Education: The politics and practice of formative assessment*, London: RoutledgeFalmer.

Elliott, G. (1996a) *Crisis and Change in Vocational Education and Training*, London: Kogan Page.

Elliott, G. (1996b) 'Why is research invisible in Further Education?', *British Education Research Journal* 22: 101–111.

Engeström, Y. (2001) 'Expansive learning at work: towards an activity-theoretical reconceptualisation', *Journal of Education and Work* 14(1): 133–156.

Fergusson, R. (1998) 'Choice, selection and the social construction of difference', in G. Hughes and G. Lewis (eds) *Unsettling Welfare: The reconstruction of social policy*, London: Routledge.

Fielding, M. (1999) 'Radical collegiality: affirming teaching as an inclusive professional practice', *Australian Educational Researcher* 26(2): 1–34.

Flyvbjerg, B. (2006) 'Five misunderstandings about case study research', *Qualitative Inquiry* 12(2): 219–245.

Foster, A. (2005) *Realising the Potential: A review of the future role of further education colleges*, Annesley, UK: DfES Publications.

Fraser, B. and Treagust, D. F. (1986) 'Validity and use of an instrument for assessing classroom psychosocial environment in higher education', *Higher Education* 15: 37–57.

Freire, P. (1972) *Pedagogy of the Oppressed*, Harmondsworth: Penguin.

Fuller, A. and Unwin, L. (2003) 'Learning as apprentices in the contemporary UK workplace: creating and managing expansive and restrictive participation', *Journal of Education and Work* 16(4): 407–426.

Fuller, A., Hodkinson, H., Hodkinson, P. and Unwin, L. (2005) 'Learning as peripheral participation in communities of practice: a reassessment of key concepts in workplace learning', *British Educational Research Journal* 31(1): 49–68.

Furlong, J. and Oancea, A. (2005) *Assessing Quality in Applied and Practice-based Educational Research: A framework for discussion*, Oxford: Oxford University Department of Educational Studies.

Further Education Curriculum Review and Development Unit (FECRDU) (1979) *A Basis for Choice: Report of a study group on post-16 pre-employment courses*, London: FECRDU.

Further Education Unit (FEU) (1991) *Flexible Colleges: Access to learning and qualifications in further education, Part 2*, London: FEU.

Further Education Unit (1992) *Quality Education and Training for the Adult Unemployed: A manual for planners and managers in FE*, London: FEU.

Gewirtz, S. (2002) *The Managerial School*, London: Routledge.

Girard, R. (1977) *Violence and the Sacred*, Baltimore, MD: Johns Hopkins University Press.

Gleeson, D. (1999) 'Challenging tripartism: class inequality in post compulsory education policy', in J. Demaine (ed.) *Education Policy and Contemporary Politics*, London: Macmillan.

Gleeson, D. and Mardle, G. (1980) *Further Education or Training? A case study in the theory and practice of day-release education*, London: Routledge & Kegan Paul.

Gleeson, D. and Shain, F. (1999) 'Managing ambiguity: between markets and managerialism – a case study of middle managers in further education', *Sociological Review* 47: 461–490.

Gleeson, D., Davies, J. and Wheeler, E. (2005) 'On the making and taking of professionalism in the further education workplace', *British Journal of Sociology of Education* 26(4): 445–460.

Green, A. and Lucas, N. (eds) (1999) *FE and Lifelong Learning: Re-aligning the sector for the twenty-first century*, Bedford Way Papers, London: Institute of Education.

Grenfell, M. and James, D. (with Hodkinson, P., Reay, D. and Robbins, D.) (1998) *Bourdieu and Education: Acts of practical theory*, London: Falmer Press.

Grenfell, M. and James, D. (2004) 'Change in the field-changing the field: Bourdieu and the methodological practice of educational research', *British Journal of Sociology of Education* 25(4): 507–523.

Guile, D. and Lucas, N. (1999) 'Rethinking initial teacher education and professional development in Further Education: towards the learning professional', in A. Green and N. Lucas (eds) *FE and Lifelong Learning: Realigning the sector for the twenty-first century*, Bedford Way Papers, London: Institute of Education.

Hammersley, M. (1997) 'Educational research and teaching: a response to David Hargreaves's TTA lecture', *British Educational Research Journal* 23(2): 141–162.

Hammersley, M. (2002) *Educational Research, Policymaking and Practice*, London: Paul Chapman.

Hammond, M. (2001) 'Key skills: a metamorphosis of failure?', paper presented at the Fifth Annual Conference of the Learning and Skills Research Network, Robinson College, University of Cambridge, December.

Hargreaves, D. (1996) 'Teaching as a research-based profession: possibilities and prospects', Teacher Training Agency Annual Lecture, London.

Hargreaves, D. (1997) 'In defence of research for evidence-based teaching: a rejoinder to Martyn Hammersley', *British Educational Research Journal* 23: 405–420.

Hayward, G., Hodgson, A., Johnson, J., Oancea, A., Pring, R., Spours, K., Wilde, S. and Wright, S. (2005) *Nuffield Review of 14–19 Education and Training, Annual Report 2004–05*, Oxford: University of Oxford Department of Educational Studies.

Heathcote, G., Kempa, R. and Roberts, I. (1982) *Curriculum Styles and Strategies*, London: Further Education Unit.

Hey, V. and Bradford, S. (2004) 'The return of the repressed? The gender politics of emergent forms of professionalism in education', *Journal of Education Policy* 19(6): 691–713.

Hillage, J., Pearson, R., Anderson, A. and Tamkin, P. (1998) *Excellence in Schools*, London: Institute for Employment Studies.

Hochschild, A.R. (1983) *The Managed Heart: Commercialization of human feeling*, Berkeley, CA: University of California Press.

Hodkinson, H. and Hodkinson, P. (2004) 'Rethinking the concept of community of practice in relation to schoolteachers' workplace learning', *International Journal of Training and Development* 8(1): 21–31.

Hodkinson, P. (2004) 'Research as a form of work: expertise, community and methodological objectivity', *British Educational Research Journal* 30(1): 9–26.

Hodkinson, P. and Bloomer, M. (2000) 'Stokingham Sixth Form College: institutional culture and dispositions to learning', *British Journal of Sociology of Education* 21: 187–202.

Hodkinson, P. and Smith, J.K. (2004) 'The relationship between educational research, policy and practice: improving understanding and judgement making', in R. Pring and G. Thomas (eds) *Evidence Based Practice in Education*, Buckingham: Open University Press.

Hodkinson, P., Anderson, G., Colley, H., Davies, J., Diment, K., Scaife, T., Tedder, M., Wahlberg, M. and Wheeler, E. (2004) 'Learning cultures in Further Education', paper presented at the Annual Conference of the British Educational Research Association, UMIST, Manchester, September.

Holly, M.L. (1984) *Keeping a Personal-Professional Journal*, Geelong, Victoria: Deakin University.

Hughes, C., Taylor, P. and Tight, M. (1996) 'The ever-changing world of Further Education: a case for research', *Research in Post Compulsory Education* 1: 7–18.

Hyland, T. (1997) 'Reconsidering competence', *Journal of Philosophy of Education* 31(3): 491–503.

Hyland, T. and Merrill, B. (2003) *The Changing Face of Further Education: Lifelong learning, inclusion and community values in further education*, London: RoutledgeFalmer.

IfL (2006) Institute for Learning website homepage http://www.ifl.ac.uk/ (accessed November 2006).

James, D. (1995) 'Mature studentship: beyond a "species" approach', *British Journal of Sociology of Education* 16(4): 451–466.

James, D. (ed.) (2004) *Research in Practice: Experiences, insights and interventions from the project Transforming Learning Cultures in Further Education*, London: Learning and Skills Research Council.

James, D. (2005) 'Importance and impotence? Learning, outcomes and research in further education', *The Curriculum Journal* 16(1): 83–96.

James, D. and Diment, K. (2002) 'HNC Engineering case study', unpublished TLC Project Working Paper.

James, D. and Diment, K. (2003) 'Going underground? Learning and assessment in an ambiguous space', *Journal of Vocational Education and Training* 55(4): 407–422.

James, M., Pollard, A., Rees, G. and Taylor, C. (2005) 'Researching learning outcomes: building confidence in our conclusions', *The Curriculum Journal* 16(1): 109–122.

James, N. (1989) 'Emotional labour: skill and work in the social regulation of feelings', *Sociological Review* 37: 15–42.

Jessup, G. (1991) *Outcomes: NVQs and the emerging model of education and training*, London: Falmer Press.

Lave, J. (1996) 'Teaching, as learning, in practice', *Mind, Culture and Society* 3(3): 149–164.

Lave, J. and Wenger, E. (1991) *Situated Learning: Legitimate peripheral participation*, Cambridge: Cambridge University Press.

Lawn, M. and Ozga, J. (1988) 'The educational worker? A reassessment of teachers', in J. Ozga (ed.) *Schoolwork: Approaches to the labour process of teaching*, Milton Keynes: Open University Press.

Lea, J., Hayes, D., Armitage, A., Lomas, L. and Markless, S. (2003) *Working in Post-compulsory Education*, Maidenhead: Open University Press.

Learning and Skills Council (LSC) (2002) *Student Numbers at Colleges in the Further Education Sector and External Institutions in England on 1 November 2001* (Statistical First Release 21), London: LSC.

Learning and Skills Council (2005) Learner Numbers. Available at http://www. lsc.gov.uk/cgi-bin/MsmGo.exe?grab_id=2&EXTRA_ARG=&host_id= 42&page_id=1379840&query=sfr&hiword=sfr+ (Index of Statistical First Releases) (accessed May 2005).

Learning and Skills Development Agency (LSDA) (2003) Research contractors registration. Available at www.lsda.org.uk/research/contractors/ (accessed September 2006).

Leathwood, C. (2005) '"Treat me as a human being – don't look at me as a woman": femininities and professional identities in further education', *Gender and Education* 17(4): 387–409.

Leitch, S. (2006) *Prosperity for All in the Global Economy: World class skills*, Final Report, London: HM Treasury.

LLUK (2006) Lifelong Learning UK website homepage http://www.lluk.org/ (accessed November 2006).

Mackney, P. (2004) 'Opinion', *Guardian*, 5 May: 15.

Malcolm, J. and Zukas, M. (2000) 'Constructing pedagogic identities: versions of the educator in adult and higher education', *Proceedings of 41st Adult Education Research Conference*, Vancouver: University of British Columbia.

Miliband, D. (2006) 'Public services and public goods: lessons for reform', speech by Rt Hon David Miliband MP at the National School of Governance conference, Queen Elizabeth II Conference Centre, London, 6 June. Available at http://www.defra.gov.uk/corporate/ministers/speeches/david-miliband/ dm060606.htm (accessed July 2006).

Moore, R. (1984) 'Schooling and the world of work', in I. Bates, J. Clarke, P.

Cohen, D. Finn, R. Moore and P. Willis (eds) *Schooling for the Dole? The new vocationalism*, London: Macmillan.

National Association of Teachers in Further and Higher Education (NATFHE) (1983) *Future Trends in F&HE: A discussion paper*, London: NATFHE.

Oakley, A. (2000) *Experiments in Knowing: Gender and method in the social sciences*, London: Polity Press.

Payne, J. (1999) 'All things to all people: changing perceptions of "skill" among Britain's policy makers since the 1950s and their implications', SKOPE Research Paper no. 1, University of Warwick.

Postlethwaite, K. and Maull, W. (2003) 'Similarities and differences amongst learning sites in four Further Education colleges in England, and some implications for the transformation of learning cultures', *Journal of Vocational Education and Training* 55(4): 447–469.

Postlethwaite, K. and Maull, W. (2007) 'Changing learning environments: factors affecting change in learning sites in four FE Colleges in England', *Educational Review* (in press).

Power, M. (1997) *The Audit Society: Rituals of verification*, Oxford: Oxford University Press.

Pursaill, J. (1989) *National Vocational Qualifications and Further Education: A commentary on progress*, London: Further Education Unit.

Quality Improvement Agency (QIA) (2006) QIA website homepage. Available at http://www.qia.org.uk (accessed 20 June 2006).

Ranson, S. (2003) 'Public accountability in the age of neo-liberal governance', *Journal of Education Policy* 18(5): 459–480.

Reay, D. (2001) 'The paradox of contemporary femininities in education: combining fluidity with fixity', in B. Francis and C. Skelton (eds) *Investigating Gender: contemporary perspectives in education*, Buckingham: Open University Press.

Reynolds, D. (1998) 'Teacher effectiveness: better teachers, better schools', Teacher Training Agency Annual Lecture, reprinted in *Research Intelligence* 66(October): 26–29.

Riddell, S., Barron, S. and Wilson, A. (2006) *Lifelong Learning, Learning Difficulties and the Learning Society*. Available at http://www.gla.ac.uk/disabilityresearch/lifelong_learning_profile.htm (accessed September 2006).

Robertson, S. (2003) 'WTO/GATS and the global education services industry', *Globalisation, Societies and Education* 1(3): 259–266.

Russell, T.J. (1981) *Curriculum Control: A review of the major styles of curriculum design in FE*, Bristol: Further Education Curriculum Review and Development Unit/Coombe Lodge.

Sayer, A. (2005) *The Moral Sigificance of Class*, Cambridge: Cambridge University Press.

Scaife, T. (2004) 'The culture of the now: barriers to research in FE', paper presented at the Annual Conference of the Yorkshire and Humberside Learning and Skills Research Network, Leeds, July.

Sfard, A. (1998) 'On two metaphors for learning and the dangers of choosing just one', *Educational Researcher* 27(2): 4–13.

Shain, F. (2000) 'Managing to lead: women managers in the further education sector', *Journal of Further and Higher Education* 24(2): 173–201.

Shain, F. and Gleeson, D. (1999) 'Under new management: changing conceptions of teacher professionalism and policy in the further education sector', *Journal of Education Policy* 14: 445–462.

Silver, H. (1988) *Intentions and Outcomes: Vocationalism in further education*, London: Longman and Further Education Unit.

Simons, H., Kushner, S., Jones, K. and James, D. (2003) 'From evidence-based practice to practice-based evidence: the idea of situated generalisation', *Research Papers in Education* 18(4): 347–364.

Skeggs, B. (1997) *Formations of Class and Gender: Becoming respectable*, London: Sage.

Smith, D.E. (1999) *Writing the Social: Critique, theory and investigations*, Toronto: University of Toronto Press.

Smith, M.J. (2000) *Culture: Reinventing the social sciences*, Buckingham: Open University Press.

Stanton, G. and Bailey, B. (2004) 'Fit for purpose? Sixty years of VET policy in England', in G. Hayward and S. James (eds) *Balancing the Skills Equation: Key issues and challenges for policy and practice*, Bristol: Policy Press.

Stenhouse, L. (1975) *An Introduction to Curriculum Research and Development*, London: Heinemann.

Stokes, D.E. (1997) *Pasteur's Quadrant: Basic science and technological innovation*, Washington, DC: Brookings Institution.

Stronach, I. and Morris, B. (1994) 'Polemical notes on educational evaluation in the age of "policy hysteria"', *Evaluation and Research in Education* 8(1–2): 5–18.

Stronach, I., Corbin, B., Mcnamara, O., Stark, S. and Warne, T. (2002) 'Towards an uncertain politics of professionalism: teacher and nurse identities in flux', *Journal of Education Policy* 17(1): 109–138.

Tarrant, J. (2000) 'What is wrong with competence?' *Journal of Further and Higher Education* 24(1): 77–83.

Taylor, P. (1993) *The Texts of Paulo Freire*, Buckingham: Open University Press.

Taylor, P.C., Fraser, B. and Fisher, P.A. (1997) 'Monitoring constructivist classroom learning environments', *International Journal of Educational Research* 27(4): 293–302.

Tedder, M. (2002) 'BTEC National Diploma in Health Studies case study 2', unpublished TLC Project Working Paper.

Tooley, J. and Darby, D. (1998) *Education Research: An OFSTED critique*, London: Office for Standards in Education.

Torrance, H., Colley, H., Ecclestone, K., Garratt, D., James, D., Jarvis, J. and Piper, H. (2005) *The Impact of Different Modes of Assessment on Achievement and Progress in the Learning and Skills Sector*, London: LSDA.

Unwin (2002) '21st century vocational education in the UK: what would Dickens think?' Inaugural lecture, Centre for Labour Market Studies, University of Leicester.

Vandenberghe, F (2000) '"The real is relational": an epistemological analysis of Pierre Bourdieu's generative structuralism', in D. Robbins (ed.) *Pierre Bourdieu*, Vol. 2, London: Sage.

Vanderstraeten, R. and Biesta, G.J.J. (2006) 'How is education possible? A pragmatist account of communication and the social organisation of education', *British Journal of Educational Studies* 54(2): 160–174.

Venables, E. (1968) *Leaving School and Starting Work*, Oxford: Pergamon.

Vianna, E. and Stetsenko, A. (2006) 'Embracing history through transforming it', *Theory and Psychology* 16(1): 81–108.

Wahlberg, M. and Gleeson, D. (2003) '"Doing the business": paradox and irony in vocational education – GNVQ Business Studies as a case in point', *Journal of Vocational Education and Training* 55(4): 423–445.

Walkerdine, V. (2003) 'Reclassifying upward mobility: femininity and the neo-liberal subject', *Gender and Education* 15(3): 237–248.

Wallace, M. and Hoyle, E. (2005) 'Towards effective management of a reformed teaching profession', paper presented to ESRC Teaching and Learning Research Programme thematic seminar series Changing Teacher Roles, Identities and Professionalism, King's College London, July. Available at http://www.kcl.ac.uk/content/1/c6/01/41/66/paper-wallace.pdf (accessed September 2006).

Wenger, E. (1998) *Communities of Practice: Learning, meaning, and identity*, Cambridge: Cambridge University Press.

Wertsch, J.V. (1998) *Mind as Action*, New York: Oxford University Press.

Williams, R. (1983) *Keywords: A vocabulary of culture and society*, revised edition, Oxford: Oxford University Press.

Working Group on 14–19 Reform (2004) *14–19 Curriculum and Qualifications Reform: Final report of the Working Group on 14–19 Reform*, Tomlinson Report, Annesley, UK: DfES Publications.

Index

Lightning Source UK Ltd.
Milton Keynes UK
UKOW020905280112

186216UK00010B/14/P